McGraw-Hill Education

500 Evolve Reach (HESI) A2 Questions to Know by Test Day

D0595204

McGraw-Hill Education

500 Evolve Reach (HESI) A2 Questions to Know by Test Day

Kathy A. Zahler, MS

New York   Chicago   San Francisco   Athens   London   Madrid
Mexico City   Milan   New Delhi   Singapore   Sydney   Toronto

1 2 3 4 5 6 7 8 9 0   QFR/QFR   1 2 1 0 9 8 7 6 5

ISBN   978-0-07-184772-8
MHID   0-07-184772-3

e-ISBN   978-0-07-184773-5
e-MHID   0-07-184773-1

McGraw-Hill Education books are available at special quantity discounts to use as premiums and sales promotions or for use in corporate training programs. To contact a representative, please visit the Contact Us pages at www.mhprofessional.com.

CONTENTS

INTRODUCTION

Congratulations! You've taken a big step toward success on the HESI A2 by purchasing *McGraw-Hill Education: 500 Evolve Reach (HESI) A2 Questions.* We are here to help you take the next step and score high on your exam so you can get into the nursing school of your choice.

Based on *McGraw-Hill's 3 Evolve Reach (HESI) A2 Practice Tests,* this book presents practice questions from that popular study guide and adds more than 200 brand-new ones so you can focus on problem-solving. These 500 HESI A2-style questions cover the key concepts found on the exam. Most of these questions are multiple-choice, but a few, the numeric entry questions under Basic Math Skills, ask for a specific answer. Each question is clearly explained in the answer key. The questions will give you valuable independent practice to supplement your earlier review.

This book and the others in the series were written by expert authors who know the subject inside and out and can identify crucial information as well as the kinds of questions that are most likely to appear on the exam.

You might be the kind of student who needs a few weeks of extra study before the exam for a final review. Or you might be the kind of student who puts off preparing until the last minute before the exam. No matter what your preparation style, you will benefit from reviewing these 500 questions, which closely parallel the content and degree of difficulty of the questions on the actual HESI A2 exam. These questions and the explanations in the answer key are the ideal last-minute study tool for those final weeks before the test.

If you practice with all the questions and answers in this book, we are certain you will build the skills and confidence needed to excel on your test. Good luck!

—The Editors of McGraw-Hill Education

CHAPTER 1

Reading Comprehension

Concussion

A concussion is a traumatic injury to the brain that can interfere with the way the brain processes information and functions. A concussion often results in severe headaches, diminished alertness, and even unconsciousness.

While over one million people in the United States suffer concussions every year, many believe that, like people, no two concussions are identical. Recently two professional baseball players suffered concussions. The first player was injured early in the season, tried twice to return to regular play, but was not medically cleared to play until the following year. Even after eight months, this player reported a recurring condition of "fogginess" that seemed to linger. The second player had brief symptoms of sleepiness and involuntary movement, or "shakiness." A few days later, and after several tests, the second player reported that the effects of the concussion had subsided, and was cleared to play.

No matter the duration of a person's recovery, refraining from trying to do too much, too soon is vital. A specialist at Boston University's Center for the Study of Traumatic Encephalopathy believes that someone who suffers a second concussion while still recovering from the first risks an even longer recovery.

Full recovery from concussions is possible. Problems are seldom permanent and, for most people who have had a concussion, the long-term prognosis is typically excellent. The first baseball player recently returned to his team. And though he was told by his physician that he has no greater risk than anyone else of suffering another concussion, other physicians believe that suffering one sports-related concussion increases the likelihood of suffering another.

1. Which of the following is *not* listed as a detail in the passage?
    (A) Football and lacrosse players suffer the most concussions.
    (B) Over a million Americans a year suffer concussions.
    (C) Concussions may result in diminished alertness.
    (D) It may take longer to recover from a second concussion.

2. What is the meaning of the word *diminished* as used in the first paragraph?

(A) Miniature
(B) Reduced
(C) Recurrent
(D) Hollow

3. Choose the best summary of the passage.

(A) No two concussions are alike. Some people may recover easily from concussion while others may take weeks or months. In any case, receiving a second concussion too soon may mean a lengthy recovery.
(B) When baseball players receive concussions, some take a long time to recover. Some may try to return to play too soon and receive a second concussion that ends their career.
(C) Although most athletes shrug off concussions, they would be wise to take them seriously. Multiple concussions can cause serious harm to the brain, which is rattled around in the skull with each injury.
(D) Recovery from concussion is possible, but it is not always a good idea to return to play too soon. Some head injuries are called concussions but do not really qualify as such.

4. What is the author's primary purpose in writing this essay?

(A) To entertain
(B) To analyze
(C) To reflect
(D) To inform

5. Which statement would *not* be inferred by the reader?

(A) Athletes should be careful after a first concussion.
(B) Severe headache after a fall may be a sign of concussion.
(C) Sports-related concussions are riskier than other kinds.
(D) Symptoms of concussion may linger for over six months.

Obsession Plus Addiction

It is hard to imagine how the eating disorders anorexia and bulimia could be any worse than they already are, but somehow people have found a way. Known unofficially as *drunkorexia,* this condition is a blend of self-imposed starvation or binging and purging mixed with alcohol abuse. Anorexics use alcohol either to soothe their conscience for eating something they feel they should not, or as their only sustenance. Bulimics binge on alcohol for emotional reasons and then purge by vomiting all of it back up.

Our current culture's obsession with thinness, coupled with widespread acceptance of drug and alcohol abuse, has made this combination particularly attractive. Dr. Doug Bunnell, former president of the National Eating Disorders

Association, said, "Binge drinking is almost cool and hip, and losing weight and being thin is a cultural imperative for young women in America. Mixing both is not surprising, and it has reached a tipping point in terms of public awareness."

Some experts are beginning to explore the possible psychological and neurological links between eating disorders and substance abuse. Does eating or binging somehow trigger the same pleasure centers as drugs or alcohol? Another avenue being explored is what to do if a person has both conditions.

Treatment for addiction is abstinence, but no one can abstain completely from food. As Dr. Kevin Wandler, vice president for medical services at an eating disorders center, phrases it, "Eating normally would be an effective behavior, but it's easier to give up alcohol and drugs because you never need them again. If your drug is food, that's a challenge."

6. Identify the overall tone of the essay.
   (A) Dismayed
   (B) Fascinated
   (C) Reassured
   (D) Suspicious

7. What is the meaning of the word *abstain* as used in the last paragraph?
   (A) Dishonor
   (B) Go without
   (C) Connect to
   (D) Liberate

8. Which of the following is *not* listed as a detail in the passage?
   (A) Anorexics' use of alcohol as sustenance
   (B) Bulimics' use of alcohol for emotional reasons
   (C) Cultural reasons for drunkorexia
   (D) Medical cures for drunkorexia

9. What is the author's primary purpose in writing this essay?
   (A) To inform
   (B) To persuade
   (C) To entertain
   (D) To analyze

Sunnyside Up

Most people are familiar with the damaging effects of the sun on unprotected skin, but not enough attention is paid to the many positive effects of receiving direct exposure to sunlight on a regular basis.

The most compelling argument for increased exposure to sunlight is the need for vitamin D in the human body. Vitamin D is integral for maintaining healthy bones and preventing diseases like rickets and osteoporosis. It is synthesized by the skin when it comes into contact with the UVB rays found in sunlight. In order to ensure you are receiving the proper amount of vitamin D, it is recommended to get 15 minutes of direct exposure to sunlight at least two or three times a week. UVB rays are made less intense when passing through clouds and pollution, and will not transmit through glass or sunscreen. UVB rays are also less effective the further in distance you are from the equator. People with darker skin require more exposure to the sun to receive the same amount of vitamin D.

In addition to vitamin D, sunlight will help regulate the circadian rhythms that ensure you get a good night's sleep. Sunlight helps to prevent an overactive immune system, which may prove useful in preventing autoimmune diseases like psoriasis and lupus. Recent studies have even shown that sunlight can help lessen the symptoms of Alzheimer's disease.

The negative impacts of excess exposure to sunlight should not be ignored; cancers resulting from skin damage are a real concern that must be taken seriously. But the importance of vitamin D and the other positive impacts of sunlight make a compelling argument for making sure we are spending enough time every week in direct sunlight.

10. What is the main idea of the passage?

   (A) There are many positive effects of receiving direct exposure to sunlight.
   (B) The negative impacts of sunlight should not be ignored.
   (C) Vitamin D is integral for maintaining healthy bones and preventing diseases.
   (D) Vitamin D is synthesized by our bodies in reaction to direct sunlight.

11. The term *compelling*, as used in the second paragraph, can best be defined as _____.

   (A) reasonable
   (B) convincing
   (C) common
   (D) worthwhile

12. What is the author's primary purpose in writing this essay?

   (A) To persuade
   (B) To reflect
   (C) To entertain
   (D) To analyze

13. Identify the overall tone of the essay.
    (A) Confused
    (B) Confident
    (C) Disheartened
    (D) Disapproving

14. Choose the best summary of the passage.
    (A) Light-skinned people need a maximum of 15 minutes a day in direct sunlight to achieve the benefits of the sun's rays. Dark-skinned people may need far more time in the sun to reap the same benefits.
    (B) Spending too much time indoors can wreak havoc with your circadian rhythms, leach vitamin D from your bones, and damage your immune system. Exercising outdoors in direct sunlight or in a room with clear glass is recommended.
    (C) Although negative effects of sunlight are well known, people should be aware that some sunlight is necessary and beneficial. Exposure to sunlight increases vitamin D, improves sleep, and prevents hyperactivity of the immune system.
    (D) You can avoid direct sunlight but still reap the benefits of a day in the sun by using sunscreen or tinted glass. The effects of vitamin D are beneficial, so it is wise to spend some time outdoors while fully protected from the dangerous rays.

Eating Local Foods

If you spend every Saturday at your local farmers' market, picking over the beans and radishes, you are participating in a popular pastime that has enormous benefits for your community and your health. A study from Michigan State University suggests a variety of reasons to buy your food locally.

Support for your local economy and environment makes buying locally an obvious plus. Why wouldn't you want your hard-earned dollars to go to farmers and growers from your own community? Why wouldn't you want to help those farmers to retain their land, which provides your home town or region with open space and acres of greenery?

You have probably had the experience of buying tomatoes in winter and finding that they are tasteless and hard. When we eat locally, we eat foods in their season, meaning that we eat them at the peak of flavor and ripeness. Shipping fruits or vegetables from somewhere in South America means that they are picked before they are ripe and may lose most of their nutrients by the time they reach your local grocery. In winter, a large percentage of the produce you see in the grocery comes from locations hundreds of miles away.

The Michigan State study also points out the hazards involved in eating food from far away. If vegetables or meat travel from place to place before arriving at your grocery store, they have multiple opportunities to become contaminated.

A sign on blueberries showing that they are grown at Fairhaven Farm allows you to do a bit of research on that farm to discover how they grow their blueberries. Do they spray them with pesticides? Do they pick fresh berries daily? When you buy at the farmers' market, you often have the opportunity to ask the farmer directly about the food you are about to consume.

15. The word *retain*, as used in the second paragraph, most closely means
____.

    (A) contain
    (B) keep
    (C) cultivate
    (D) buy up

16. What is the author's purpose in writing this essay?

    (A) To entertain
    (B) To reflect
    (C) To evaluate
    (D) To persuade

17. Choose the best summary of the passage.

    (A) The benefits of eating locally include support for the local economy and environment as well as better taste, nutrition, and safety.
    (B) People who buy and eat local foods will see improvement in their health through eating uncontaminated, ripe fruits and vegetables.
    (C) Farmers benefit when people eat locally, which helps to pump needed dollars into the local economy.
    (D) Today's shipping of vegetables and fruits from far away means that they lose nutritional value and are likely to be unripe and tasteless.

18. Which of the following statements is the author's opinion?

    (A) A study from Michigan State University suggests a variety of reasons to buy your food locally.
    (B) Support for your local economy and environment make buying locally an obvious plus.
    (C) In winter, a large percentage of the produce you see in the grocery comes from locations hundreds of miles away.
    (D) The Michigan State study also points out the hazards involved in eating food from far away.

19. Which of the following is a conclusion that a reader can draw from this passage?

(A) Locally grown produce tastes better than produce that is shipped from far away.

(B) Everyone should take the time to plant a small garden plot and grow vegetables.

(C) Farmers' markets would be more helpful if they were open every week all year round.

(D) Vegetables and fruits should be purchased locally, but meat may come from far away.

Yoga

Yoga is an exercise that everyone should try. Yoga was first practiced thousands of years ago. It helps connect the mind and body by taking a person through a series of poses while emphasizing controlled breathing and meditation. Every year hundreds of thousands of people enjoy the benefits of yoga by treating the movements and postures as exercise.

Yoga works by safely stretching muscles, ligaments, and tendons. This helps release the buildup of lactic acid in the muscles that can often cause stiffness, tension, and even pain. Yoga helps develop the body's range of mobility and increases the ease of everyday movements. Many participants report improved flexibility, especially in the trunk and shoulders, after only two months of practice. Yoga improves posture, balance, and sleep, and it also helps with weight control.

Physically, many yoga poses help build upper-body strength, which is increasingly important as the body ages. Other poses help strengthen the muscles in the lower back, and when properly practiced, nearly all of the poses strengthen the body's abdominal, or core, muscles. This helps improve the circulation of blood that increases the delivery of nutrients and oxygen to the body, and also removes wastes produced by the body. When combined with yoga's benefit of lowering a person's heart rate, the result is increased cardiovascular endurance.

The University of Maryland School of Nursing recently published a study that showed yoga was especially effective at reducing stress. In addition, researchers found that yoga surpassed traditional aerobic exercise, often significantly, in improving flexibility, pain tolerance, and daily energy levels. One enthusiast says that her advice to skeptics is simple, "Take a deep breath, stretch, and indulge in a few poses. You'll feel better."

20. Identify the overall tone of the essay.

(A) Earnest

(B) Negative

(C) Self-satisfied

(D) Skeptical

21. What is the meaning of the word *tolerance* as used in the last paragraph?
    (A) Open-mindedness
    (B) Approval
    (C) Endurance
    (D) Generosity

22. The passage lists all of these benefits of yoga *except* _____.
    (A) improved circulation
    (B) strengthening of core muscles
    (C) stress reduction
    (D) fortification of immune system

23. What is the author's primary purpose in writing this essay?
    (A) To persuade
    (B) To entertain
    (C) To analyze
    (D) To reflect

Hypothermia in Infants

Hypothermia is a condition in which the body loses heat faster than it produces heat. Someone your age may end up with hypothermia from being outside on a frosty day for hours without adequate warm clothing. An elderly person may develop the condition after sitting in an air conditioned room for a prolonged period of time. However, hypothermia in infants is the most common of all, and potentially the most dangerous.

Infants lose body heat faster than adults do. They have a higher ratio of surface area (skin) to volume, so cold on the outside is more easily turned into cold on the inside, which can be dangerous. In addition, they are unable to use shivering to keep themselves warm, meaning that they burn fat instead. That fact can mean that a baby kept in cold temperatures will grow at a slower rate than a baby who is warm.

Signs of hypothermia in infants include red skin (especially on the extremities) that is cold to the touch, low energy, weak crying, and failure to eat. The baby should be rewarmed and then kept in warmer clothing away from air conditioning or drafts. Carrying the baby next to the parent in a kangaroo-style sling is one means of keeping him or her warm. When that is not possible, dressing the infant in a warm onesie with socks and a hat can suffice. Never cover a newborn with multiple blankets; instead, dress the baby appropriately to maintain a normal body temperature.

New parents would be wise to remember that the newborn has spent nine months in a moist climate with temperatures ranging in the high 90s. Napping by the window on a pleasant 80-degree day can feel shockingly cold to that newborn.

24. Which of the following is a conclusion that a reader can draw from this passage?

    (A) Babies born in summer have an advantage over babies born in colder months.
    (B) A baby with red skin on the arms and legs should immediately be rewarmed.
    (C) Babies are more sensitive to changes in temperature than adults are.
    (D) Parents of newborns are unaware of the dangers of open windows and air conditioning.

25. Identify the overall tone of the essay.

    (A) Annoyed
    (B) Respectful
    (C) Fascinated
    (D) Cautionary

26. Which of the following is *not* listed as a detail in the passage?

    (A) Elderly people are also prone to hypothermia.
    (B) Blue lips are one sign that a child is too cold.
    (C) Slings are one means of keeping small babies warm.
    (D) You should never put a baby under heavy blankets.

27. The word *suffice*, as used in paragraph 3, most closely means _____.

    (A) oversee
    (B) make sure of
    (C) be enough
    (D) check up on

28. Which statement would *not* be inferred by the reader?

    (A) Shivering is a learned response that infants do not have.
    (B) Keeping a newborn warm is a critical task of new parents.
    (C) Serious hypothermia can be a life-or-death issue for infants.
    (D) Certain low-weight infants may be too cold to thrive.

Aromatherapy—Fact or Fiction?

For years, aromatherapy has been touted as a safe and natural way to relax and even heal. Essential oils from a variety of scents have been added to candles and sprays to help people feel better. However, a recent study performed at Ohio State University says that these smells, as nice as they may be, do not do a thing to improve people's health.

To find out if aromatherapy actually works, the researchers tested two of the most popular scents: lemon and lavender. First, test subjects had their heart rate, blood pressure, stress hormones, and immune function measured and noted. Next, they were subjected to mild stressors and then told to sniff one of the scents to see if the scent would help them to relax. Finally, all the subjects were tested again to look for improvement. There were no significant changes noted—even in people who had previously stated they were true believers in the power of aromatherapy.

Of course, this does not necessarily prove that aromatherapy is worthless, either. It was just one small study, pitted against the opinions of thousands of consumers who swear by peppermint on their pillow for an upset stomach or vanilla for a headache. More tests will be done, but in the meantime, a whiff of lavender, lemon, or other scents will certainly do no harm—and can be quite pleasant at the same time.

29. Which of the following is a conclusion that a reader can draw from this passage?

    (A) Aromatherapy is not a legitimate therapy by anyone's standards.
    (B) Lemon and lavender are not healthy scents to inhale or use.
    (C) More studies are needed to determine if aromatherapy is truly beneficial.
    (D) Adding aromatherapy to regular treatment will help speed healing.

30. What is the meaning of the word *touted* as used in the first paragraph?

    (A) Revealed
    (B) Glorified
    (C) Overcome
    (D) Deceived

31. Identify the overall tone of the essay.

    (A) Congratulatory
    (B) Uncertain
    (C) Annoyed
    (D) Distressed

32. Which of the following is *not* listed as a detail in the passage?

    (A) Subjects were given mild stressors.
    (B) Lemon and lavender scents were tested.
    (C) Vanilla worked better than lemon for stress.
    (D) The study took place at Ohio State University.

Electronic Health Records

In 2009, the HITECH Act was signed into law as a means of encouraging widespread use of electronic health records. This reflected the ongoing movement of industry and government into computerization of recordkeeping, and it transformed many hospitals and clinics into nearly paperless offices.

One goal of electronic health records (EHRs) is to produce one seamless record for each patient that follows that patient around the health care system. Records might include vital signs, medical history, immunizations, blood work, symptoms, allergies, and so on. This information may then be shared among organizations, so that an elderly patient X who starts in surgery may have records sent easily to a rehabilitation facility and then to home health care and the patient's local pharmacy. This can ensure that everyone dealing with patient X is on the same page when it comes to his care, and it eliminates the need for multiple printouts or faxes.

A well-constructed EHR system includes tools for clinical decision support (CDS), so that a physician may quickly search for specific information that applies to a given patient. Knowing that patient X is allergic to certain antibiotics, for example, the physician may easily access a list of alternatives that would be appropriate for post-surgical care.

A third aspect of EHRs is the computerized physician order entry (CPOE). Through this system, physicians may transmit orders to the nursing staff, physical therapists, pharmacists, and so on. Estimates indicate that computerizing orders using standardized wording and abbreviations may reduce medication errors by as much as 80 percent.

No system is foolproof, and EHRs may be costly and difficult to initiate. The information within the system is only as good as the people who enter it. However, all indications are that organizations with strong EHRs are more efficient and less accident-prone than those that still use paper.

33. The word *seamless* in the second paragraph most closely means _____.

    (A) unified
    (B) perfect
    (C) stitched
    (D) paperless

34. What is the main idea of the passage?

    (A) Many hospitals and clinics are using EHRs instead of paper records, but progress is slow.
    (B) Along with EHRs, health care organizations may use CPOEs and tools for CDS.
    (C) EHRs can make it easier to communicate, record, and maintain patient records.
    (D) Without good EHRs, medical personnel are more likely to make critical errors.

35. Which of the following statements is an opinion?

(A) In 2009, the HITECH Act was signed into law as a means of encouraging widespread use of electronic health records.

(B) Records might include vital signs, medical history, immunizations, blood work, symptoms, allergies, and so on.

(C) A third aspect of EHRs is the computerized physician order entry (CPOE).

(D) No system is foolproof, and EHRs may be costly and difficult to initiate.

36. What conclusion can you draw from the first sentence of paragraph 2?

(A) Transportation of patients is one important factor controlled by EHRs.

(B) Before EHRs, a patient might have multiple records kept by multiple doctors.

(C) Patients will now be served by a single physician or medical group instead of many.

(D) The health care system too often loses track of a patient who moves within the system.

37. Which of the following is *not* listed as a detail in the passage?

(A) The kinds of records that might make up an EHR.

(B) Current percentages of medical facilities using EHRs.

(C) The kinds of workers who might receive doctors' orders.

(D) Estimates of the reduction in human error with computerized orders.

Studying Alzheimer's

Years of research have proven that Alzheimer's disease, along with other types of dementia, elevates the risk of dying early in the majority of patients. In a recent study performed by the Institute of Public Health at the University of Cambridge, scientists set out to determine just exactly how long people were likely to survive following the onset of dementia.

Currently, approximately 24 million people throughout the world suffer from the memory loss and orientation confusion that comes with Alzheimer's disease and other forms of dementia. That number appears to double every 20 years, and experts predict that by the year 2040, there will be 81 million people living with some level of the condition. The more researchers and doctors can learn about what causes the problem, as well as how to treat it, the better prepared they will be to handle these millions of future patients.

To determine how people's life spans are affected by this medical condition, the scientists studied 13,000 seniors for a period of 14 years. During that time, 438 people developed dementia, the vast majority of whom died. The factors of age, disability, and gender were analyzed to see how they affected longevity as well.

Conclusions from the study showed that women tended to live slightly longer than men, averaging 4.6 years from the onset of dementia, as opposed to 4.1 years for men. The patients who were already weak or frail at the onset of dementia died first, regardless of age. Marital status, living environment, and degree of mental decline, although relevant factors, were not shown to be influential.

Researchers from the University of Cambridge hope that this new information will help patients, clinicians, care providers, service providers, policymakers, and others who deal with dementia. The more they know, the better they will be able to respond to this heartbreaking condition.

38. What is the main idea of the passage?

   (A) More than 24 million people suffer from some form of dementia.
   (B) A recent study looked at the longevity of dementia sufferers.
   (C) Women with dementia live slightly longer than men do.
   (D) Dementia is a heartbreaking disease that is hard on families.

39. What is the meaning of the word *onset* as used in the first paragraph?

   (A) Cure rate
   (B) Incubation period
   (C) Remainder
   (D) Commencement

40. What is the author's primary purpose in writing this essay?

   (A) To persuade
   (B) To entertain
   (C) To inform
   (D) To analyze

41. Identify the overall tone of the essay.

   (A) Anxious
   (B) Irate
   (C) Indifferent
   (D) Sympathetic

42. Choose the best summary of the passage.

   (A) Marital status, age, and gender seem not to be issues in the longevity of patients who suffer from dementia. Out of 438 people with dementia, the vast majority were dead within a few years.
   (B) In hopes of discovering information that can assist with care for dementia patients, Cambridge researchers studied 13,000 seniors. They found that dementia sufferers lived on average slightly over four years.
   (C) Alzheimer's is just one form of dementia, a medical condition that affects millions and whose prevalence is expected to increase greatly over the next few decades.
   (D) Researchers at Cambridge University have discovered that men with dementia live longer than women with the condition, but frailty is a definite indicator of an early death in patients with dementia.

Underage Drinkers and TV Ads

A recent study from Johns Hopkins indicates a strong correlation between television advertising for alcohol and the drinking behavior of underage youth. It appears that young people are three times more likely to drink brands they see advertised on television compared to other brands, regardless of price or other factors.

The study has many calling for a reduction of exposure of young people to alcohol advertising, just as people insisted on removal of cigarette advertising from television back in 1970. In that year, the Public Health Cigarette Smoking Act banned any such ads on radio or television and required stronger health warnings on packaging.

Will the current study lead to a similar ban for alcohol? It would be a hard sell for the television industry. Right now, it is estimated that close to half of all ads teenagers see on television are for alcohol. In the first four months of 2014 alone, Bud Light spent $84.3 million on television ads, and the beer industry as a whole spent close to half a billion.

At present, the only regulation on alcohol advertising is self-regulation. Many beer companies and vodka manufacturers include ads urging moderation. However, the message that young people receive, despite the industry's seemingly good intentions, is that buying that brand is a good idea.

Earlier studies have shown that exposure to alcohol advertising increases the likelihood that young people will drink. This study expands on that by showing that what they will drink is motivated by the ads themselves. Young people are brand-conscious, and given the choice, they will go with the brand that they have seen associated with people or images that appeal to them.

43. What is the author's primary purpose in writing this essay?
    (A) To inform
    (B) To entertain
    (C) To reflect
    (D) To persuade

44. Which of the following is *not* mentioned as a result of the Public Health Cigarette Smoking Act?
    (A) Banning of radio ads
    (B) Banning of print ads
    (C) Banning of television ads
    (D) Requirement of stronger warnings

45. What does the word *moderation* mean in paragraph 4?
    (A) Normality
    (B) Compromise
    (C) Calmness
    (D) Self-restraint

46. What is the main idea of the passage?

    (A) Young adults drink more when they are watching television.
    (B) The brands young people drink are driven by the ads they see.
    (C) Keeping beer ads off television will prevent underage drinking.
    (D) Liquor ads should be banned just as cigarette ads once were.

47. Which statement would *not* be inferred by the reader?

    (A) Only beer advertising has an ill effect on young viewers.
    (B) Young people seem to be extremely brand-conscious.
    (C) The TV industry would be likely to fight a ban on alcohol ads.
    (D) Cigarette ads do not appear on American television.

MRSA

Methicillin-resistant *Staphylococcus aureus* (MRSA) is a form of the *Staphylococcus aureus* bacterium that is resistant to antibiotics, and as a result is very difficult to treat. MRSA now kills more Americans every year than HIV/AIDS, and the rates of infection are rising.

Methicillin is an antibiotic that was introduced in the 1960s as a way of combating the *Staphylococcus aureus* bacterium that is ubiquitous in hospitals. Within a year, doctors began finding strains of bacteria that had already developed immunity to methicillin. By the 1990s, MRSA had become the leading hospital-acquired skin infection in the United States. At the same time MRSA started appearing outside of hospitals. These were different strains of the bacteria, but just as dangerous, and spreading just as quickly. In the past 15 years, MRSA bacteria have become ubiquitous not only in hospitals, but in gyms, locker rooms, swimming pools, and any other settings where human contact is common.

Researchers in Ireland are developing a technology that may significantly halt the spread of the hospital-associated MRSA bacteria. They have developed a textile consisting of nanomaterials 1,000 times smaller than a human hair; these textiles are shown to halt the spread of infection and can be used for linens, drapes, and upholstery in hospitals. The potential for this technology to reduce the instances of hospital-associated MRSA is staggering.

You can reduce your risk for community-associated MRSA infection by regularly washing your hands, covering all open wounds with a clean bandage, and not sharing any personal items such as razors or towels.

48. As used in the second paragraph, what does the term *ubiquitous* mean?

    (A) Indigenous
    (B) Often ignored
    (C) Found everywhere
    (D) Dangerous

49. What is the main idea of the passage?

(A) Methicillin may prove to be the best way to keep MRSA from killing more hospital patients.

(B) A new textile is the best bet to protect hospital patients against the dangers of MRSA.

(C) There are many different strains of MRSA, but only one is potentially fatal.

(D) MRSA is a scourge both in and out of hospitals, but there may be ways to reduce the risk.

50. Which of the following statements is an opinion?

(A) Hand-washing stations are one means of combatting MRSA infection.

(B) Not all *Staphylococcus* bacteria are resistant to antibiotics.

(C) Hospitals in the United States should quickly adopt the use of new germ-fighting textiles.

(D) MRSA infection kills more people in the United States than does HIV/AIDS.

51. Which statement would *not* be inferred by the reader?

(A) Hospitals may soon limit the spread of infection with a new textile.

(B) MRSA begins by infecting the skin.

(C) You are most likely to contract MRSA in a crowded location.

(D) Used clothing stores may harbor MRSA.

Ebola, 2014

The Ebola outbreak of 2014 was the most devastating since the virus was first described in 1976. Not only were more people affected, but the geographic boundaries of the outbreak were enormous. The virus attacked people in four African countries by July of that year—Sierra Leone, Guinea, Liberia, and Nigeria.

Ebola is known and feared for its morbidity figures—about 60 percent of all who contract the infection will die. The current virus, *Zaire ebolavirus*, is even deadlier, with a kill rate of 80 to 90 percent. Other viruses are as harmful, but none work more quickly.

The only good thing about Ebola is that it is fairly difficult to catch. It does not spread through the air, but it may spread via bodily fluids, whether directly (touching a wound) or indirectly (handling bedding or bandages).

Early symptoms include fever, headache, and vomiting. This progresses rapidly in most cases to external and internal bleeding. Ebola seems to knock out the human immune system quite quickly, and people who do not survive die from multiple organ failure, usually within six days to two weeks of showing initial symptoms.

Although there is reasonable fear that Ebola may spread across continents, it has yet to do so. Modern transportation makes pandemics more and more likely, but Ebola spreads only once a person shows symptoms. Someone that visibly sick would not be allowed on an airplane. Nevertheless, someone who is infected but as yet asymptomatic may fly. Once symptoms begin, people need to recognize quickly that the patient has been in a country with Ebola. The patient may then quickly be quarantined in an isolation unit at a hospital, protecting the general public from infection.

52. Which of the following is *not* mentioned as a symptom of Ebola infection?

  (A) Fever
  (B) Vomiting
  (C) Organ failure
  (D) Skin eruption

53. Identify the tone of the final paragraph.

  (A) Alarmist
  (B) Reproachful
  (C) Reassuring
  (D) Woeful

54. Based on this passage, what conclusion can a reader draw about Ebola?

  (A) It is difficult to contract but devastating once the infection starts.
  (B) It requires heroic measures to keep the infection from spreading.
  (C) More people die of Ebola than of any other known virus.
  (D) As of 2014, Ebola was found only in four African countries.

55. Which statement about Ebola is a fact?

  (A) A high mortality rate and lack of a cure make Ebola terrifying.
  (B) Ebola kills more rapidly than any other known virus.
  (C) External bleeding is the most dreadful part of the disease.
  (D) An Ebola pandemic is unlikely to happen in our lifetime.

56. Which is the best title for this passage?

  (A) "Return of an Ancient Disease"
  (B) "Ebola: From Africa to America"
  (C) "Scientists Look for a Cure for Ebola"
  (D) "A Deadly Outbreak of a Dreaded Virus"

An Old Form of Running Is New Again

Barefoot running is a rapidly growing movement that encourages people to leave their shoes at home and take to the streets in only their bare feet. Barefoot running advocates are quick to point out that while shoe technology has advanced significantly since the advent of the modern running shoe, there has been little decline in the amount of injuries that occur from running.

Humankind has been running for millions of years, and modern running shoes have existed for less than 50 years. By wearing larger shoes with excessive cushioning we are changing the biomechanics of how we run, thereby increasing the likelihood for injury. Early humans ran with a "forefoot strike," landing closer to the balls of their feet and using their foot's natural arch as a spring to store and release energy. Modern shoe designs encourage a "heel strike," landing on the heel and rolling forward to the toe. Barefoot running advocates believe "heel striking" replaces your reliance on the natural mechanics of your feet with the cushioning provided by your shoes, and that this is what causes many of the injuries affecting runners today.

Critics assert that while our feet may have been designed for barefoot running, our road surfaces were not. Concrete and asphalt are much firmer than any surface where our human ancestors would have been running. Broken glass and debris also may make barefoot running a significant challenge.

There is little consensus when it comes to the safety and effectiveness of barefoot running, but even the most skeptical of podiatrists will agree that wearing heavily padded shoes too often can result in a weaker foot and leg structure. Spend some extra time walking barefoot around your house; aside from building up the muscles and tendons that strengthen your feet, you may just find yourself tempted to go for a run.

57. Which might be a good title for this passage?
    (A) "Everyone Should Run Barefoot"
    (B) "How to Prevent Running Injuries"
    (C) "Modern Road Surfaces vs. Barefoot Running"
    (D) "The Debate over Barefoot Running"

58. What is the meaning of the word *consensus* as it is used in the last paragraph?
    (A) Investigation
    (B) Purpose
    (C) Trepidation
    (D) Unanimity

59. Which statement would *not* be inferred by the reader?
    (A) Runners who take their shoes off may face some hazards.
    (B) Modern running shoes may increase the odds for injury.
    (C) Walking barefoot is good for the muscles and tendons.
    (D) Before 1950, even Olympic runners ran barefoot.

60. Which of the following statements is an opinion?

    (A) Running barefoot is natural and advantageous.

    (B) The cost of modern running shoes keeps increasing.

    (C) Concrete sidewalks are harder than dirt paths.

    (D) The arch of the foot gives a spring to the step.

Forensic Nursing

Forensic nursing is a specialty that may appeal to someone who is fascinated by the criminal justice system and wants to be a part of it while exercising particular nursing skills. Forensic nurses may work at all points in a criminal investigation, with different specialists working on different aspects.

Some forensic nurses work with victims. Sexual assault nurse examiners assess a victim's injuries, perform rape kit exams and otherwise collect evidence, and provide referrals to counseling or further medical care. Forensic gerontology specialists assist with cases of elder abuse or neglect. Often they work in nursing homes or hospitals, providing expertise to other staff members. Forensic clinical nurse specialists train and consult in emergency rooms or on death investigation teams. Nurse coroners arrive early on at the scene of a suspicious death and examine the body to determine time and possible cause of death.

Other forensic nurses work with the accused. Correctional nursing specialists work with people in correctional facilities from juvenile hall to prison. They may administer medication, perform physical examinations, or care for ill prisoners.

Still other forensic nurses work with the courts. In a civil case where medical knowledge is needed, a legal nurse consultant may assist attorneys in analyzing evidence or serving as a liaison between lawyers and doctors. Cases involving medical malpractice or personal injury suits may require a nurse's expertise and assistance. Nurses may also be used to assist the legal community in family court cases of child abuse or domestic violence.

Forensic nurses typically handle the usual course load of nursing courses but will also need coursework in law enforcement, forensic science, mental health, and special populations. Many people who choose this specialty have worked as nurses for a while already. Often emergency room nurses or critical care nurses find that their work with victims is so satisfying that they wish to pursue this specialization.

61. What is the main idea of the passage?

    (A) Forensic nursing is a specialty that merges the worlds of health and law.

    (B) Forensic nurses often train for years before deciding that this specialty is for them.

    (C) Forensic nurses work with victims, often people who have been abused or injured.

    (D) More and more nursing programs are offering a popular specialization, forensic nursing.

62. A reader may infer that forensic nurses who work with the accused typically step in _____.
    (A) for cases of neglect
    (B) with legal assistance
    (C) at the scene of a crime
    (D) after sentencing

63. What is the meaning of the word *pursue* as it is used in the final paragraph?
    (A) Take up
    (B) Track down
    (C) Stick to
    (D) Result in

64. Which is *not* mentioned as a type of case that might involve the assistance of a legal nurse consultant?
    (A) Medical malpractice case
    (B) Personal injury suit
    (C) Nursing home elder abuse case
    (D) Domestic violence case

65. Identify the overall tone of the essay.
    (A) Neutral
    (B) Energized
    (C) Skeptical
    (D) Concerned

CHAPTER 2

Vocabulary and General Knowledge

66. Select the meaning of the underlined word in the sentence.

He is a <u>prolific</u> scientist, generating several important studies each year.

(A) Productive
(B) Influential
(C) Valuable
(D) Respected

67. What is the meaning of *vacuous*?

(A) Tired
(B) Restful
(C) Clean
(D) Empty

68. If a nurse is *circumspect* with patient records, what is she doing?

(A) Evaluating them
(B) Guarding them
(C) Presenting them
(D) Disputing them

69. To *stanch* a wound is to _____ it.

(A) inflict
(B) restrict
(C) examine
(D) enfold

70. What is the meaning of *ostracize*?

(A) Snub
(B) Hide from
(C) Condescend to
(D) Hire

71. Select the meaning of the underlined word in the sentence.

The hospital accepts a certain quota of <u>indigent</u> patients.

(A) Impoverished
(B) Resentful
(C) Apathetic
(D) Uninjured

72. A *nit* is a kind of _____.

(A) abscess
(B) parasite
(C) bandage
(D) infection

73. What is the meaning of *augment*?

(A) Add to
(B) Hash out
(C) Sell off
(D) Make difficult

74. Select the meaning of the underlined word in the sentence.

The patients are under <u>quarantine</u> until further notice.

(A) A specialist's care
(B) Experimental drug therapy
(C) Imprisonment in a rehabilitation unit
(D) Confinement away from the general population

75. Which word names a medicine whose purpose is to induce vomiting?

(A) Opiate
(B) Narcotic
(C) Emetic
(D) Prophylactic

76. What is another word for *panacea*?

(A) Clinician
(B) Painkiller
(C) Vista
(D) Cure

77. Which word refers to the surgical removal of an organ's contents?

(A) Vivisection
(B) Amputation
(C) Evisceration
(D) Augmentation

78. What is another word for *flux*?

(A) Quantity
(B) Discharge
(C) Inflation
(D) Strength

79. What is the meaning of *regulations*?

(A) Movements
(B) Supervisors
(C) Rules and laws
(D) Government officials

80. A patient who is *querulous* might be guilty of _____.

(A) overeating
(B) questioning
(C) complaining
(D) stealing

81. What is the meaning of *pernicious*?

(A) Destructive
(B) Valued
(C) Finicky
(D) Perpetual

82. Select the meaning of the underlined word in the sentence.

The night nursing staff is <u>accountable</u> for those records.

(A) Receptive
(B) Notorious
(C) Responsible
(D) Preoccupied with

83. A blood vessel that is *distended* is _____.

(A) overturned
(B) swollen
(C) twisted
(D) overlong

84. Something that is *viscous* is thick and sticky. Another word for this might be _____.

(A) fluid
(B) molten
(C) gelatinous
(D) malleable

85. What is the meaning of *collusion*?

(A) Slander
(B) Assortment
(C) Accident
(D) Conspiracy

86. If a theory is *obsolete*, what is true of it?

(A) It makes sense.
(B) It is inflexible.
(C) It is outdated.
(D) It was never true.

87. A patient who is *lethargic* may seem _____.

(A) agitated
(B) anguished
(C) disorganized
(D) exhausted

88. What does *onerous* mean?

(A) Authentic
(B) Burdensome
(C) Honorable
(D) Biased

89. Someone who is *altruistic* might also be called _____.

(A) transformed
(B) clichéd
(C) primitive
(D) charitable

90. Select the meaning of the underlined word in the sentence.

The students observed the tricky procedure with a certain amount of trepidation.

(A) Eagerness
(B) Misgivings
(C) Expertise
(D) Disbelief

91. What is the meaning of *precept*?

(A) Guiding principle
(B) Fractional part
(C) Clear understanding
(D) Local district

92. A *truculent* patient is _____.

    (A) fatigued
    (B) irresponsible
    (C) supportive
    (D) argumentative

93. If patients are being *counseled*, what is happening?

    (A) They are being comforted.
    (B) They are being advised.
    (C) They are being deceived.
    (D) They are being healed.

94. Select the meaning of the underlined word in the sentence.

    Apply the gel on the gingival <u>margin</u> around the selected teeth using the blunt-tipped applicator included in the package.

    (A) Edge
    (B) Grease
    (C) Incisor
    (D) Cavity

95. If a patient has *sallow* skin, what is true?

    (A) Her skin has a yellow tint.
    (B) Her skin is loose.
    (C) Her skin is dry and flaky.
    (D) Her skin is thin and taut.

96. If a doctor has an *exemplary* record, her work is _____.

    (A) instructive
    (B) expressive
    (C) praiseworthy
    (D) methodical

97. What is the meaning of *nebulous*?

    (A) Jolly
    (B) Hesitant
    (C) Vague
    (D) Approximate

98. The voice box may be called the _____.

    (A) larynx
    (B) lynx
    (C) pharynx
    (D) phalanx

99. Select the meaning of the underlined word in the sentence.

The interns observed the <u>contours</u> of the patient's rash.

(A) Shape
(B) Answers
(C) Amount
(D) Extension

100. What is the meaning of *incorrigible*?

(A) Clever
(B) Potential
(C) Incurable
(D) Undistinguished

101. If a patient's condition is *deteriorating,* he is _____.

(A) getting worse
(B) improving gradually
(C) resisting medication
(D) failing to eat or drink

102. *Precipitous* is best defined as being _____.

(A) damp
(B) gentle
(C) swift
(D) dull

103. Select the meaning of the underlined word in the sentence.

Being overweight may <u>predispose</u> a person to diabetes.

(A) Make susceptible
(B) Bring to light
(C) Save from harm
(D) Pass over

104. What is the meaning of *soporific*?

(A) Very sweet
(B) Inducing sleep
(C) Half awake
(D) Immature

105. If someone is *disseminating* information, what is he doing?

(A) Broadcasting it
(B) Assessing it
(C) Contradicting it
(D) Influencing it

106. If you are described as an *assiduous* worker, you are probably _____.

    (A) unreliable
    (B) experienced
    (C) industrious
    (D) inventive

107. What does *instigate* mean?

    (A) Instruct
    (B) Connect
    (C) Reproduce
    (D) Activate

108. Select the meaning of the underlined word in the sentence.

This medication works by <u>inhibiting</u> the action of a certain enzyme.

    (A) Occupying
    (B) Speeding
    (C) Hindering
    (D) Enhancing

109. A symptom that is *exacerbated* is _____.

    (A) not dangerous
    (B) disfiguring
    (C) painful
    (D) made worse

110. To *critique* something is to _____.

    (A) appraise it
    (B) condemn it
    (C) extol it
    (D) berate it

111. What is the meaning of *contrite*?

    (A) Regretful
    (B) Limited
    (C) Gratified
    (D) Distasteful

112. Select the meaning of the underlined word in the sentence.

Her <u>guileless</u> manner is one of her most noticeable qualities.

    (A) Remorseful
    (B) Insightful
    (C) Courteous
    (D) Straightforward

113. What does *redundancy* mean?

(A) Observation
(B) Surplus
(C) Consequence
(D) Patrol

114. A body part that has *atrophied* has _____.

(A) darkened
(B) withered
(C) blistered
(D) fragmented

115. *Anterior* refers to which part of the human body?

(A) Top
(B) Bottom
(C) Front
(D) Back

116. What is the best description for the term *gravid*?

(A) Deadly serious
(B) Expecting a child
(C) Germ-free
(D) Diseased

117. Select the meaning of the underlined word in the sentence.

The cavity, once opened, proved to be <u>riddled</u> with infection.

(A) Challenged
(B) Overrun
(C) Separated
(D) Complete

118. If a treatment *mitigates* symptoms, the symptoms become _____.

(A) less severe
(B) masked
(C) curable
(D) lingering

119. What does the word *banal* mean?

(A) Simple
(B) Notable
(C) Ordinary
(D) Past

120. The *ramifications* of a course of treatment are that treatment's _____.

(A) costs
(B) consequences
(C) barriers
(D) phases

121. What does *respite* mean?

(A) Kindness
(B) Effect
(C) Worry
(D) Relief

122. What is another word for *asymmetric*?

(A) Proportionate
(B) Impartial
(C) Uneven
(D) Magnified

123. What is the meaning of *counterfeit*?

(A) Over-the-counter
(B) Foreign
(C) Fake
(D) Unidentified

124. What is the best description for the word *efficacy* in this sentence?

The quality, safety, and efficacy of the new medicines are not known.

(A) Effectiveness
(B) Significance
(C) Corollary
(D) Conclusion

125. What is the meaning of *debilitating*?

(A) Regenerating
(B) Amplifying
(C) Incapacitating
(D) Disheartening

126. A surgeon who is *adroit* might be described as _____.

(A) admired
(B) scholarly
(C) sophisticated
(D) skillful

127. What does *torpid* mean?

    (A) Sticky
    (B) Sluggish
    (C) Stifling
    (D) Reckless

128. Select the meaning of the underlined word in the sentence.

    Did the interns <u>contravene</u> the doctor's orders?

    (A) Comply with
    (B) Misjudge
    (C) Comprehend
    (D) Disregard

129. *Caudal* refers to which part of the human torso?

    (A) Top
    (B) Bottom
    (C) Front
    (D) Back

130. What is the best description for the term *aseptic*?

    (A) Combined
    (B) Purified
    (C) Sedating
    (D) Tainted

CHAPTER 3

Grammar

131. Which word is used incorrectly in the following sentence?

After rapidly consume that enormous meal, he felt a bit dyspeptic.

(A) rapidly
(B) consume
(C) felt
(D) dyspeptic

132. What punctuation is needed in this sentence to make it correct?

Dr. Abrams came here from England he has only been in Delaware for one year.

(A) Comma
(B) Semicolon
(C) Colon
(D) Hyphen

133. Select the word that makes this sentence grammatically correct.

Few students were able to complete the assignment in the allotted time; _____, the professor gave them an additional week in which to do the work.

(A) despite
(B) in fact
(C) therefore
(D) conversely

134. What word is best to substitute for the underlined words in the following sentence?

You can hear <u>the nurses'</u> laughter all the way down the hallway.

(A) his
(B) hers
(C) them
(D) their

135. Which word is used incorrectly in the following sentence?

Moving stealthy, the sneaky little boy reached up for the cookie jar on the topmost shelf.

(A) stealthy
(B) sneaky
(C) up
(D) topmost

136. Which sentence is the clearest?

(A) I saw the criminals who were arrested on the TV news.
(B) I saw the criminals on the TV news who were arrested.
(C) On the TV news, the criminals who were arrested were seen by me.
(D) On the TV news, I saw the criminals who were arrested.

137. Which word is *not* spelled correctly in the context of the sentence?

Our mayer made a proclamation declaring that all citizens must recycle.

(A) mayer
(B) proclamation
(C) citizens
(D) recycle

138. Select the word or phrase that will make the sentence grammatically correct.

Jennifer must _____ been confused by the complicated directions.

(A) of
(B) had
(C) have
(D) be

139. Which of the following is spelled correctly?

(A) Seisure
(B) Siezure
(C) Seizher
(D) Seizure

140. Select the phrase or clause that is misplaced in the sentence.

Accompanied by toast, Jake enjoyed his farm-fresh eggs and sweet-tasting grits.

(A) Accompanied by toast
(B) Jake enjoyed
(C) farm-fresh eggs
(D) sweet-tasting grits

141. Select the word that makes this sentence grammatically correct.

After _____ the course, the nursing students will take a short practicum.
- (A) finished
- (B) finishing
- (C) having finish
- (D) will finish

142. What punctuation is needed in this sentence to make it correct?

"Please dont be afraid to ask questions," she assured us politely.
- (A) Period
- (B) Quotation marks
- (C) Comma
- (D) Apostrophe

143. Which word is *not* spelled correctly in the context of the sentence?

The pharmacist seemed to disagree with the proscription designated by the physician.
- (A) pharmacist
- (B) proscription
- (C) designated
- (D) physician

144. What punctuation is needed in this sentence to make it correct?

Have you finished reading the lab results so we can schedule an appointment with the patient
- (A) Period
- (B) Question mark
- (C) Comma
- (D) Semicolon

145. Which of the following is spelled correctly?
- (A) Discipline
- (B) Disipline
- (C) Discapline
- (D) Dicipline

146. Which sentence is grammatically correct?

(A) The new employees watched a short training film following a session with the hospital administrator.

(B) A session with the hospital administrator was followed by a short training film by the new employees.

(C) Following a session with the hospital administrator, a short training film was watched by the new employees.

(D) Following a session with the hospital administrator, the new employees watched a short training film.

147. Which word is spelled correctly?

(A) Noticable

(B) Notisable

(C) Noticeable

(D) Noticeabel

148. Select the phrase or clause that is misplaced in the sentence.

I did not see the open carton of orange juice on the shelf standing with the refrigerator door open.

(A) I did not see

(B) of orange juice

(C) on the shelf

(D) standing with the refrigerator door open

149. Select the word or phrase that will make the sentence grammatically correct.

Do not be afraid to consult _____ your peers.

(A) with

(B) from

(C) by

(D) in

150. Which sentence is clearest?

(A) The soup was hot and made of tomatoes; Dan burned his tongue and gulped some cold water.

(B) After burning his tongue on the hot tomato soup, Dan gulped some cold water.

(C) Dan gulped some cold water when the tomato soup that was hot burned his tongue.

(D) Gulping some cold water, Dan burned his tongue on the hot tomato soup.

151. Which word is spelled correctly?

(A) Controversial
(B) Contraversial
(C) Contravercial
(D) Contriversal

152. Which word is used incorrectly in the following sentence?

Exercising excessively can have significant nugatory effects.

(A) excessively
(B) significant
(C) nugatory
(D) effects

153. Select the word that makes this sentence grammatically correct.

The committee finished _____ report in time for the annual review.

(A) its
(B) their
(C) it's
(D) they're

154. What punctuation is needed in this sentence to make it correct?

Courtney ran around the track and her roommates kept track of her time.

(A) Period
(B) Comma
(C) Colon
(D) Apostrophe

155. Which of the following is spelled correctly?

(A) Insessant
(B) Incesant
(C) Incessent
(D) Incessant

156. Select the correct word for the blank in the following sentence.

We were not sure to _____ we should give the paperwork.

(A) who
(B) whoever
(C) whom
(D) whomever

157. What punctuation is needed in this sentence to make it correct?

Mrs. Alvarez showed us three possibilities for the anteroom walls flowered wallpaper, striped wallpaper, or stippled paint.

(A) Comma
(B) Semicolon
(C) Colon
(D) Hyphen

158. Select the word that makes this sentence grammatically correct.

Having _____ one pill at bedtime, the patient was able to sleep for eight hours.

(A) took
(B) take
(C) taking
(D) taken

159. Which sentence is grammatically correct?

(A) Tapping the beat, Ms. Schuster led the chorus in song.
(B) Ms. Schuster led the chorus in song tapping the beat.
(C) Ms. Schuster led the chorus, tapping the beat, in song.
(D) Tapping the beat, the chorus was led in song by Ms. Schuster.

160. Select the word that makes this sentence grammatically correct.

One out of four doctors _____ to this plan.

(A) subscribe
(B) subscribes
(C) subscribing
(D) are subscribed

161. Which of the following words is spelled correctly?

(A) Proffesional
(B) Proffessional
(C) Profesional
(D) Professional

162. What punctuation is needed in this sentence to make it correct?

I did not entirely understand his instructions; nevertheless I attempted to hook up the computer on my own.

(A) Comma
(B) Semicolon
(C) Dash
(D) Period

163. Select the correct word for the blank in the following sentence.

We _____ never been trained in that particular procedure.

(A) has
(B) was
(C) had
(D) will

164. Which sentence is written correctly?

(A) When he told you to mark his words did you assume he meant that you should pay attention?
(B) When he told you to "mark his words" did you assume he meant that you should pay attention?
(C) When he told you to "mark his words" did you assume he meant that "you should pay attention"?
(D) When he told you to mark his words, did you assume he meant that you should pay attention?

165. Which word is used incorrectly in the following sentence?

The couple is extraordinarily gifted, and their prodigy have benefited from the brainpower of their forebears.

(A) extraordinarily
(B) prodigy
(C) brainpower
(D) forebears

166. Which word is *not* spelled correctly in the context of the sentence?

Nothing can be more delightful then a late-night swim in the reservoir.

(A) Nothing
(B) delightful
(C) then
(D) reservoir

167. What punctuation is needed in this sentence to make it correct?

Although we had met earlier the busy doctor could not recall my name.

(A) Period
(B) Question mark
(C) Comma
(D) Semicolon

168. Which of the following is spelled correctly?

(A) Labertory
(B) Laberatory
(C) Labratory
(D) Laboratory

169. Which sentence is written correctly?

(A) Rebecca has read that novel twenty times, astonishingly, she still finds it entertaining.
(B) Rebecca has read that novel twenty times; astonishingly, she still finds it entertaining.
(C) Rebecca has read that novel twenty times astonishingly; she still finds it entertaining.
(D) Rebecca has read that novel twenty times, astonishingly she still finds it entertaining.

170. Which sentence is clearest?

(A) The geese were flying south in a V formation with hikers on the mountain spotting them.
(B) As the geese flew south, hikers were on the mountain, spotting the geese in a V formation.
(C) Hikers on the mountain spotted geese flying south in a V formation.
(D) In a V formation, geese flying south spotted hikers on the mountain.

171. Which word is used incorrectly in the following sentence?

The professor was formally an intern in this very hospital back in the 1980s.

(A) professor
(B) formally
(C) intern
(D) very

172. Select the correct word for the blank in the following sentence.

The children and _____ performed a skit for the elderly patients.

(A) he
(B) me
(C) them
(D) her

173. Select the sentence that is grammatically correct.

(A) The office of finances had sent him a message reminding him to pay his tuition bill.

(B) The office of finances send him a message reminding him to pay his tuition bill.

(C) The office of finances have sent him a message reminding him to pay his tuition bill.

(D) The office of finances sent him a message reminds him to pay his tuition bill.

174. Select the word that makes this sentence grammatically correct.

If you will _____ down here, the doctor will check your flexibility.

(A) set
(B) seat
(C) lay
(D) lie

175. Which of the following is spelled correctly?

(A) Mechanical
(B) Mechanicle
(C) Mecanical
(D) Machinical

176. Which sentence is written correctly?

(A) Since completing the technical course Jasper has had several offers.

(B) Since completing the technical course, Jasper has had several offers.

(C) Since completing, the technical course, Jasper has had several offers.

(D) Since completing the technical course; Jasper has had several offers.

177. Select the word or phrase that makes this sentence grammatically correct.

There is a fountain _____ the driveway and the main entrance.

(A) among
(B) between
(C) by way of
(D) in conjunction with

178. Which word is used incorrectly in the following sentence?

The doctor's spear of influence includes most people working in the disciplines of neurology and pain management.

(A) spear
(B) influence
(C) disciplines
(D) management

179. Which of the following words is spelled correctly?

(A) Irrelevant
(B) Irelevant
(C) Irrelevent
(D) Irrellevant

180. Which sentence is written correctly?

(A) Maria has an unusual background, she started off as a student of geology.
(B) Maria has an unusual background; she started off as a student of geology.
(C) Maria has an unusual background she started off as a student of geology.
(D) Maria has an unusual background: she started off as a student of geology.

181. Select the phrase that will make this sentence grammatically correct.

Until the semester ends, Lily _____.

(A) is not traveling far from town
(B) has not traveled far from town
(C) will not have traveled far from town
(D) will not travel far from town

182. Which word is *not* spelled correctly in the context of the sentence?

The ingenuous foxes managed to lever open one side of the coop.

(A) ingenuous
(B) foxes
(C) lever
(D) coop

183. Select the word that will make this sentence grammatically correct.

You will need to choose _____ courses in biology, chemistry, and anatomy.

(A) between
(B) besides
(C) among
(D) amid

184. Which word is used incorrectly in the following sentence?

Jeremiah seemed enthusiastically when we reported on our astonishing success.

(A) seemed
(B) enthusiastically
(C) astonishing
(D) success

185. Select the sentence that is grammatically correct.

(A) Kindly hand the keys over to him and me.
(B) Kindly hand the keys over to him and I.
(C) Kindly hand the keys over to me and him.
(D) Kindly hand the keys over to he and I.

186. What word is best to substitute for the underlined word in the following sentence?

Could Kendra manage to carry both Kendra's books and yours?

(A) her
(B) his
(C) she's
(D) hers

187. Which of the following words is spelled correctly?

(A) Prefferential
(B) Preferential
(C) Preferencial
(D) Preferrencial

188. What punctuation is needed in this sentence to make it correct?

Follow my lead I have been performing this procedure for years.

(A) Period
(B) Comma
(C) Question mark
(D) Semicolon

189. Select the phrase that will make this sentence grammatically correct.

When the lecture was over, two students _____.

(A) raise their hands to ask questions
(B) raised their hands to ask questions
(C) have raised their hands to ask questions
(D) are raising their hands to ask questions

190. Which word is used incorrectly in the following sentence?

He received an oral dose initial, followed by an IV drip.
- (A) received
- (B) dose
- (C) initial
- (D) followed

191. Select the sentence that is grammatically correct.
- (A) Having replaced the broken glass, the window looked as good as new.
- (B) After the broken glass was replaced, the window looked as good as new.
- (C) Following the broken glass replacement, the window looked as good as new.
- (D) After we replaced the broken glass, the window looked as good as new.

192. Select the word that makes this sentence grammatically correct.

She was the _____ speaker I had ever heard in my years at the clinic.
- (A) inspirational
- (B) more inspirational
- (C) most inspirational
- (D) most inspirationalest

193. Which of the following words is spelled correctly?
- (A) Debenare
- (B) Debbinair
- (C) Debonare
- (D) Debonair

194. What punctuation is needed to make this sentence correct?

Jacob was delighted to be bumped up to the first class cabin on the overseas flight.
- (A) Comma
- (B) Hyphen
- (C) Dash
- (D) Apostrophe

195. Which sentence is written correctly?
- (A) "Is our state's per-capita Medicare spending in line with the national average," he asked?
- (B) "Is our state's per-capita Medicare spending in line with the national average?" He asked.
- (C) "Is our state's per-capita Medicare spending in line with the national average"? he asked.
- (D) "Is our state's per-capita Medicare spending in line with the national average?" he asked.

CHAPTER 4

Basic Math Skills

196. Beatrice purchased some dishes at the tag sale for $.75 apiece. If she paid with a $10 bill and received $1.75 in change, how many dishes did she purchase? (Enter numeric value only.)

_____

197. Add and simplify: $\frac{1}{3} + \frac{1}{4} + \frac{1}{5} =$

(A) $\frac{4}{5}$
(B) $\frac{13}{15}$
(C) $\frac{47}{60}$
(D) $\frac{83}{90}$

198. If the temperature is 41° on the Fahrenheit scale, what is it on the Celsius scale?

(A) 82°
(B) 60°
(C) 25°
(D) 5°

199. Ben is training for a marathon. If he starts running 4 miles a day in week 1 and adds 2 miles per run each week, in which week will he reach his goal of a 26-mile run?

(A) Week 10
(B) Week 12
(C) Week 14
(D) Week 16

200. Eighty percent of the class passed with a 75 or higher. If that percent equaled 24 students, how many students were in the whole class?

(A) 18
(B) 30
(C) 36
(D) 60

201. If a party planner assumes 2 bottles of sparkling water per 5 guests, how many bottles must she purchase for a party of 145?

(A) 27
(B) 36
(C) 49
(D) 58

202. Stu purchased a set of 6 cups and 6 plates at a garage sale. The cups were 25 cents apiece, and the plates were 75 cents apiece. If Stu paid with a $10 bill, how much change was he owed?

(A) $4
(B) $4.50
(C) $5
(D) $5.50

203. Express 3.08 as a fraction in lowest terms.

(A) $3\frac{8}{10}$
(B) $\frac{308}{100}$
(C) $3\frac{4}{50}$
(D) $3\frac{2}{25}$

204. Rosie made $239.98 this week working at the student union. She put half into savings to help pay her tuition and board and then spent $65 on a textbook. How much did Rosie have left from her paycheck?

(A) $54.99
(B) $64.94
(C) $87.49
(D) $184.99

205. What is 120% of 20?

(A) 24
(B) 44
(C) 140
(D) 480

206. Add and simplify: $\frac{1}{2} + \frac{1}{4} + \frac{1}{6} =$

(A) $\frac{11}{24}$
(B) $\frac{11}{12}$
(C) $\frac{3}{4}$
(D) $\frac{5}{6}$

207. Multiply: $0.12 \times 0.15 =$
(A) 0.0018
(B) 0.018
(C) 0.18
(D) 1.8

208. On the lot at Stafford Motors are 7 pickup trucks, 7 two-door automobiles, 28 four-door automobiles, and 14 SUVs. What percentage of the vehicles on the lot are SUVs? (Enter numeric value only. If rounding is necessary, round to the whole number.)

_____

209. In what numeric system does 101 name this amount: ★★★★★?
(A) Roman
(B) Arabic
(C) Decimal
(D) Binary

210. Multiply: $0.4 \times 0.05 =$
(A) 2.0
(B) 0.2
(C) 0.02
(D) 0.002

211. Write the date 1929 in Roman numerals.
(A) MCMIX
(B) MCXXIX
(C) CMXXIX
(D) MCMXXIX

212. At Jules's Grocery, Lena bought 6 apples for $5.70. How many did Sarah buy for $3.80?
(A) 2
(B) 3
(C) 4
(D) 5

213. In Juanita's nursing class, 15% of the students graduated from a two-year program. If there are 220 students in her class, how many did _not_ graduate from a two-year program?
(A) 187
(B) 160
(C) 133
(D) 35

214. How many quarts are there in 4 gallons? (Enter numeric value only.)

_____

215. Express ⅘ as a percent.

(A) 20%
(B) 40%
(C) 50%
(D) 80%

216. About how many kilometers are there in 12 miles?

(A) 7.5 miles
(B) 13.2 miles
(C) 19.2 miles
(D) 22 miles

217. What number in Arabic numerals is Roman numeral MCLXV? (Enter numeric value only.)

_____

218. Convert this military time to regular time: 1530 hours.

(A) 3:03 P.M.
(B) 3:30 A.M.
(C) 3:30 P.M.
(D) 12:30 P.M.

219. If a train travels 300 miles in 2½ hours, how far will it travel in 3 hours?

(A) 420 miles
(B) 400 miles
(C) 360 miles
(D) 320 miles

220. At the Farmer's Market, Kate bought 6 ears of corn for $.35 apiece. She paid with a $5 bill. How much change did she receive?

(A) $1.90
(B) $2.10
(C) $2.90
(D) $3.90

221. How many feet are in 6 meters?

(A) 1.83 feet
(B) 18.48 feet
(C) 18.8 feet
(D) 19.68 feet

222. Express the ratio of 25:80 as a percentage.

(A) 31.25%
(B) 34%
(C) 41.25%
(C) 43.75%

223. A package of 10 pencils is divided between every 2 students in class. If there are 20 students in class, then how many pencils are needed?

(A) 20
(B) 40
(C) 80
(D) 100

224. Subtract: $1.085 - 0.85 =$

(A) 1.0
(B) 0.935
(C) 0.235
(D) 0.215

225. Express 48% as a fraction in lowest terms.

(A) ⅗
(B) 6/7
(C) ¹²⁄₂₅
(D) ²⁴⁄₅₀

226. At Teeburg Community College, the ratio of teachers to students is 1:12. Which could be the actual student and teacher population at Teeburg?

(A) 24 teachers, 312 students
(B) 85 teachers, 1,020 students
(C) 89 teachers, 979 students
(D) 92 teachers, 1,288 students

227. Divide and simplify: $4\frac{5}{8} \div 1\frac{1}{2} =$

(A) $4\frac{1}{24}$
(B) $3\frac{23}{24}$
(C) $3\frac{1}{12}$
(D) $3\frac{1}{16}$

228. Bai Lin estimates that of her monthly paycheck, she puts 10% in savings and spends 30% on living expenses. If she has $1,545 left after that, how much is her monthly paycheck?

(A) $2,175
(B) $2,250
(C) $2,575
(D) $2,650

229. About how many pounds are there in 15 kilograms?

    (A) 20
    (B) 25
    (C) 30
    (D) 33

230. In one litter of kittens, there were 3 black kittens, 4 gray kittens, and 1 black-and-white kitten. What was the percentage of black kittens in the litter?

    (A) 50%
    (B) 48%
    (C) 37.5%
    (D) 28%

231. Subtract: $\frac{4}{7} - \frac{1}{5} =$

    (A) $\frac{13}{35}$
    (B) $\frac{11}{14}$
    (C) $\frac{3}{7}$
    (D) $\frac{3}{5}$

232. Divide: $92 \div 11 =$

    (A) 8 r3
    (B) 8 r4
    (C) 8 r7
    (D) 9 r1

233. Stanton runs 2 miles twice a week and 3 miles once a week. If he runs every week, how many miles does he run in a year?

    (A) 185
    (B) 260
    (C) 330
    (D) 364

234. What is 15 percent of 95?

    (A) 14.25
    (B) 18.5
    (C) 24.25
    (D) 28.5

235. Solve for *x*. 4 : 6 :: 120 : *x*

(A) 124

(B) 144

(C) 150

(D) 180

236. Alex is tripling a recipe that calls for a pint of cream. How much cream should he buy to ensure that he has just enough?

(A) 1 quart

(B) 1 quart and 1 pint

(C) 2 quarts

(D) 1 half gallon

237. A census of the village showed a ratio of 2:13 born-and-bred villagers to more recent arrivals. Which of the following is a possible actual number of born-and-bred villagers and more recent arrivals?

(A) 32:200

(B) 50:320

(C) 56:365

(D) 64:416

238. What percent of 84 is 126?

(A) 102%

(B) 120%

(C) 150%

(D) 175%

239. Leon bought 3 cookies for $.85 each, 2 cups of coffee for $1.49 each, and a newspaper for $1.75. He gave the cashier a $5 bill and three $1 bills. What is the greatest number of quarters he could have received as change? (Enter numeric value only.) _____

240. Multiply: 0.6 × 0.06 =

(A) 0.0036

(B) 0.036

(C) 0.36

(D) 3.6

241. If the outside temperature is currently 22 degrees on the Celsius scale, what is the approximate temperature on the Fahrenheit scale?

(A) 56° F

(B) 62° F

(C) 66.5° F

(D) 71.6° F

242. A landscaping plan is drawn on a 1:50 scale. If a deck in the plan measures 12 cm by 10 cm, how large is the deck in real life?

(A) 12 m by 10 m
(B) 6 m by 5 m
(C) 5 m by 2 m
(D) 4 m by 3 m

243. Multiply and express in lowest terms: $1\frac{2}{3} \times 3\frac{1}{2} =$

(A) $3\frac{2}{3}$
(B) $4\frac{1}{6}$
(C) $5\frac{1}{3}$
(D) $5\frac{5}{6}$

244. Sam tipped the cab driver $3.75 on a ride that cost $22. To the nearest percent, what size tip did he leave?

(A) 15%
(B) 16%
(C) 17%
(D) 18%

245. How many millimeters are there in 25 centimeters? (Enter numeric value only.) ______

246. A plan for a house is drawn on a 1:40 scale. If the length of the living room on the plan measures 4.5 inches, what is the actual length of the built living room?

(A) 45 feet
(B) 25 feet
(C) 15 feet
(D) 12 feet

247. Add: $2.34 + 23.4 + 234 =$

(A) 70.2
(B) 230.72
(C) 234.74
(D) 259.74

248. Divide and simplify: $\frac{7}{8} \div \frac{3}{8} =$

(A) $\frac{1}{2}$
(B) $1\frac{5}{8}$
(C) $2\frac{1}{8}$
(D) $2\frac{1}{3}$

249. Carlotta earned 2% on her savings of $1,050. How much did she have then?

(A) $1,052
(B) $1,060
(C) $1,071
(D) $1,075

250. Of the 300 patients receiving a placebo, 60% showed improvement in their symptoms. How many patients showed no improvement? (Enter numeric value only.)

_____

251. How many cups are there in 2 gallons? (Enter numeric value only.)

_____

252. The Myers have three sons. Jake is half as old as Tony, and Tony is 4 years younger than Quinn's age plus Jake's age. If Quinn is 10, how old is Jake?

(A) 6
(B) 8
(C) 12
(D) 16

253. Callie makes 2% interest quarterly on a deposit of $100. After a year, about how much is in her account?

(A) $102
(B) $104
(C) $106
(D) $108

254. Patient X usually ingests about 2,000 calories daily. If Patient X is placed on a regimen that cuts that daily intake by 20%, how many calories will Patient X consume in a week? (Enter numeric value only.)

_____

255. How many teaspoons are there in 3 tablespoons?

(A) 9 tablespoons
(B) 10.5 tablespoons
(C) 12 tablespoons
(D) 18 tablespoons

256. Multiply: $10.6 \times 0.3 =$

    (A) 3.08

    (B) 3.18

    (C) 3.80

    (D) 3.88

257. Of the 250 problems, Daniel got 235 correct. What grade did he receive?

    (A) 92%

    (B) 94%

    (C) 96%

    (D) 98%

258. Subtract: $43.21 - 1.234 =$

    (A) 41.976

    (B) 41.067

    (C) 30.87

    (D) 30.717

259. The number 8.4 is 15% of what number? (Enter numeric value only.)

_____

260. Add and simplify: $5\frac{2}{3} + \frac{6}{7} =$

    (A) $6\frac{1}{21}$

    (B) $6\frac{1}{7}$

    (C) $6\frac{3}{14}$

    (D) $6\frac{11}{21}$

CHAPTER 5

Biology

261. Which is an end product of digestion of carbohydrates?

   (A) Amino acids
   (B) Glucose
   (C) Fatty acids
   (D) Glycerol

262. Which is an example of an autotroph?

   (A) Algae
   (B) Fungi
   (C) Elk
   (D) Lion

263. Which gives the order of four taxonomic categories from least to most specific?

   (A) Kingdom, phylum, class, order
   (B) Kingdom, phylum, order, class
   (C) Kingdom, order, phylum, class
   (D) Kingdom, class, order, phylum

264. Which molecules contain only carbon, hydrogen, and oxygen?

   (A) Lipids and proteins
   (B) Carbohydrates and lipids
   (C) Proteins and carbohydrates
   (D) Nucleic acids and proteins

265. Which structure is found in protists but not in monerans?

   (A) Golgi apparatus
   (B) Chromosome
   (C) Cytoplasm
   (D) Cell membrane

266. How is transpiration water loss different from simple evaporation?

(A) It takes place over the ocean.
(B) It is not part of the water cycle.
(C) It is caused solely by heat.
(D) It involves plant activity.

267. Which animal breeds through internal fertilization but external development?

(A) Fox
(B) Seahorse
(C) Sparrow
(D) Earthworm

268. What happens in the kind of mutation known as an intrachromosomal translocation?

(A) A segment breaks off a chromosome and reattaches at a different point.
(B) A chromosome section or sections are attached in reverse or upside-down order.
(C) Part or all of a chromosome is added or removed.
(D) An entire section of a chromosome is duplicated and reattached.

269. In addition to lacking a nucleus, what else does a prokaryotic cell lack?

(A) Organelles
(B) Ribosomes
(C) DNA
(D) Cytoplasm

270. What kind of symbiosis exists between a pneumonia bacterium and a human?

(A) Mutualism
(B) Parasitism
(C) Commensalism
(D) Competition

271. The scientific name for a housecat is *Felis catus*. This indicates the housecat's _____ and _____.

(A) kingdom; family
(B) order; subspecies
(C) phylum; class
(D) genus; species

272. Beeswax is an example of what kind of molecule?

(A) Lipid
(B) Carbohydrate
(C) Protein
(D) Nucleic acid

273. Students grew fungi in a variety of media and measured the resulting fungi after four weeks, eight weeks, and twelve weeks. What was the independent variable in this experiment?

(A) The fungi
(B) The measurements
(C) The media
(D) The number of weeks

274. Which is *not* an organic macromolecule?

(A) Protein
(B) Nucleic acid
(C) Lipid
(D) Mineral

275. If a blood cell is placed in distilled water, what can you expect to happen?

(A) The cell will float at first and then sink.
(B) The cell will swell and blow apart.
(C) The cell will shrink and fall apart.
(D) The cell will invert and lose its shape.

276. Which is a byproduct of fermentation in muscle cells?

(A) Ethanol
(B) Pyruvic acid
(C) Lactic acid
(D) Oxygen

277. In which phase of mitosis do new nuclear membranes form around sets of chromosomes?

(A) Prophase
(B) Anaphase
(C) Telophase
(D) Interphase

278. Which option names a final step in protein synthesis?

(A) DNA unzips.
(B) Amino acids bond.
(C) Transfer RNA bonds to messenger RNA.
(D) Messenger RNA moves to ribosomes.

279. Flagella and cilia are typically used for which life process?

(A) Excretion
(B) Nutrition
(C) Respiration
(D) Movement

280. Dogs are part of a larger animal group, the Carnivora. What classification is this?

(A) Kingdom
(B) Class
(C) Order
(D) Genus

281. What are saturated fats saturated with?

(A) Hydrogen atoms
(B) Carbon atoms
(C) Oxygen atoms
(D) Nitrogen atoms

282. Which is found in animal cells but *not* in plant cells?

(A) Centriole
(B) Cytoplasm
(C) Vacuole
(D) Golgi apparatus

283. Which is a reactant in the process of photosynthesis?

(A) Glucose
(B) Oxygen
(C) Carbon dioxide
(D) Sunlight

284. Which are examples of homologous structures?

(A) Human arm and whale flipper
(B) Fish scale and bird feather
(C) Shark fin and dolphin fin
(D) Moth wing and bat wing

285. What happens to glucose during glycolysis?

(A) Its energy is entirely lost.
(B) It splits into molecules of pyruvic acid.
(C) It is stored in NADH.
(D) It joins with molecules of citric acid.

286. What process do cells in the tip of a plant's root undergo to increase in number?

(A) Meiosis
(B) Cytokinesis
(C) Oogenesis
(D) Mitosis

287. How do RNA and DNA derive their names?

(A) From the sugar each contains
(B) From the structure of their nucleotides
(C) From the information they transfer
(D) From their formative processes

288. Where does percolation take place in the water cycle?

(A) Over the ocean
(B) In a cloud
(C) Underground
(D) In a river

289. At the climax of succession in a Canadian ecosystem, what would you expect to see?

(A) Moss and lichens
(B) Grasses
(C) Large trees
(D) Shrubs

290. Which part of an animal cell contains the most water?

(A) Nucleus
(B) Cell membrane
(C) Ribosome
(D) Cytoplasm

291. Researchers are tracking changing attitudes toward solar power in northern states. Which tool would be most useful?

(A) Light meter
(B) Questionnaire
(C) Road map
(D) Solar panel

292. A naturalist observes a plant with needle-like leaves and naked seeds. Which kind of plant is it?

(A) Angiosperm
(B) Gymnosperm
(C) Fern
(D) Liverwort

293. Pupfish in the pools of Death Valley show significant differences in body shape and behavior. What is the most likely reason for this?

(A) Predation
(B) Interaction
(C) Saltation
(D) Isolation

294. Which is *not* one of the raw materials needed for cellular respiration?

(A) ADP
(B) Phosphate
(C) Water
(D) Glucose

295. Patient A, who weighs 68 kilograms, steps onto a scale 20 times. The scale consistently weighs Patient A as 75 kilograms. What is true of the measurement?

(A) It is valid, but not reliable.
(B) It is reliable, but not valid.
(C) It is both valid and reliable.
(D) It is neither reliable nor valid.

296. Which one would have the least energy efficiency in nutrient consumption?

(A) Cow
(B) Caterpillar
(C) Coyote
(D) Cricket

297. Which of these organisms has the least specialized organization?

(A) Earthworm
(B) Starfish
(C) Spider
(D) Sponge

298. A student was asked to count birds in a given location over a 24-hour period. Which count would make her data most valid?

(A) Count birds at one feeder every six hours.

(B) Count birds at three feeders at noon and 6:00 P.M.

(C) Count birds at one feeder at noon and 6:00 P.M.

(D) Count birds at three feeders every six hours.

299. How should a researcher test the hypothesis that radiation from cell phones is significant enough to raise temperature of water in a test tube?

(A) Dial a cell phone that rests beside a test tube of water, let it ring for 2 minutes, and record the temperature of the water before and after the 2-minute interval.

(B) Dial a cell phone that rests beside a test tube of water, let it ring for 2, 3, and 4 minutes, and record the temperature of the water before and after each interval.

(C) Use three different brands of cell phone; dial each as it rests beside its own test tube of water, let it ring for 2 minutes, and record the temperature of the water before and after the 2-minute interval.

(D) Use three different brands of cell phone, dial each and let one ring for 2 minutes, one for 3 minutes, and one for 4 minutes; record the temperature of the water before and after each interval.

300. Whose efficiency of energy is greater?

(A) Herbivore

(B) Carnivore

(C) Omnivore

(D) Decomposer

301. Imagine that two parents both carry the recessive gene for cystic fibrosis. Any homozygous recessive offspring will manifest the disease. What percentage of the offspring are predicted to be carriers but not manifest the disease?

(A) 0%

(B) 25%

(C) 50%

(D) 100%

302. How does the respiratory system of a frog differ from that of a human?

(A) Frogs breathe through the pores in their skin.

(B) Frogs are born with lungs but revert to gills.

(C) Frogs are born with gills but develop lungs.

(D) Frogs breathe exclusively through their gills.

303. Students believed that salt water would have a negative effect on hydra locomotion. They placed 100 hydra in a 10 percent solution of salt water and observed them over the course of a week. What was missing from their experiment?

(A) Control
(B) Hypothesis
(C) Observation
(D) Measurement

304. Which light color would be most effective for growing green plants indoors?

(A) Blue
(B) Yellow
(C) Green
(D) Orange

305. Which bacteria are spherical in shape?

(A) Clostridia
(B) Bacilli
(C) Spirilla
(D) Cocci

306. What is the term for the breakdown of glycogen into glucose subunits?

(A) Hydrolysis
(B) Reduction
(C) Metabolism
(D) Transpiration

307. Which specific genetic characteristic is unique to an individual human being?

(A) Number of chromosomes
(B) Shape of DNA
(C) Sequence of nucleotides
(D) Size of base pairs

308. Which property of water enables it to move from the roots to the leaves of a plant?

(A) Heat capacity
(B) Conductivity
(C) Solution
(D) Cohesion

309. What is required for primary active transport to take place?

(A) Potassium
(B) Sodium
(C) Glucose
(D) Chemical energy

310. Which is true of enzymes?

(A) They are made from lipids.
(B) They are made from proteins.
(C) They form double chains of DNA.
(D) They bind with catalysts.

311. Which is an example of a gymnosperm?

(A) Red cedar
(B) Japanese cherry
(C) Flowering dogwood
(D) American chestnut

312. _____ is a symbiotic relationship in which one organism benefits and the other is not affected.

(A) Mutualism
(B) Parasitism
(C) Commensalism
(D) Competition

313. Which part of a flowering plant protects the flower?

(A) Stamen
(B) Stigma
(C) Style
(D) Sepal

314. Which organism reproduces by budding?

(A) Willow
(B) Fungus
(C) Coral
(D) Fern

315. Which is a plant hormone that regulates growth and development?

(A) Tropism
(B) Auxin
(C) Petiole
(D) Chlorophyll

316. Which organelle is responsible for protein synthesis?

(A) Mitochondrion
(B) Vacuole
(C) Cell membrane
(D) Ribosome

317. Why is yeast used to make bread rise?

(A) It engages in photosynthesis, which produces oxygen gas.
(B) Carbon dioxide forms while yeast carries out photosynthesis.
(C) Yeast carries out fermentation, producing ethanol and carbon dioxide.
(D) Yeast breathes in oxygen and produces carbon dioxide through aerobic respiration.

318. How is mitosis different from meiosis?

(A) Mitosis is the process by which sex cells are formed.
(B) Meiosis creates cells with half the chromosomes of the parent cell.
(C) Telophase does not take place in mitosis.
(D) Spermatogenesis and oogenesis occur via mitosis.

319. Which one is *not* an angiosperm?

(A) Dogwood
(B) Pea plant
(C) Pear tree
(D) Ginkgo tree

320. What sort of plant growth would you expect to see in the biome known as a *taiga*?

(A) Ferns and orchids
(B) Perennial grasses
(C) Sage and scrub oaks
(D) Dense evergreen trees

321. What is represented by this formula: $6CO_2 + 6H_2O \rightarrow C6H_{12}O_6 + 6O_2$?

(A) Glycolysis
(B) Cellular respiration
(C) Photosynthesis
(D) Electronic transport

322. Three students measured the mass of a product of combustion. They recorded measurements of 5.14 g, 5.16 g, and 5.17 g. If the known mass of the product is 5.3 g, how would you describe the students' measurements?

(A) Accurate
(B) Precise
(C) Both accurate and precise
(D) Neither accurate nor precise

323. Which statement regarding energy content is true?

(A) Decomposers > secondary consumers
(B) Primary consumers > producers
(C) Producers > secondary consumers
(D) Secondary consumers > primary consumers

324. In the term *Homo sapiens*, what does *Homo* name?

(A) Class
(B) Species
(C) Genus
(D) Family

325. What is the purpose of phloem in plant tissue?

(A) To transport sugar and nutrients
(B) To assist in photosynthesis
(C) To transport water from the roots
(D) To move gases into and out of the plant

CHAPTER **6**

Chemistry

326. The difference between hydrochloric acid and hydrosulfuric acid is
_____.

    (A) that only the first is binary
    (B) that only the first is ternary
    (C) the presence of hydrogen
    (D) the nonmetallic elements in each

327. Which of these elements is a liquid at room temperature?

    (A) He
    (B) Ag
    (C) Hg
    (D) Zn

328. Which have about the same mass?

    (A) Protons and neutrons
    (B) Neutrons and electrons
    (C) Electrons and alpha particles
    (D) Neutrons and beta particles

329. Which pair are isotopes?

    (A) Co-60 and Kr-70
    (B) K-40 and Ar-40
    (C) O-15 and O-18
    (D) N-14 and C-14

330. What would you expect to happen when electrons in an excited state
fall to lower energy levels?

    (A) Energy is absorbed.
    (B) Energy is released.
    (C) Energy is both released and absorbed.
    (D) Energy remains constant.

331. Aluminum (Al) has 13 protons in its nucleus. What is the number of electrons in an Al^{3+} ion?

(A) 16
(B) 13
(C) 10
(D) 3

332. Blood with a pH of 1.3 indicates what about the blood sample?

(A) It is strongly acidic.
(B) It is strongly basic.
(C) It is weakly acidic.
(D) It is weakly basic.

333. A radioactive isotope has a half-life of 20 years. How many grams of a 6-gram sample will remain after 40 years?

(A) 8
(B) 6
(C) 3
(D) 1.5

334. What is true of a measurement in which a chemical weighs 0.031 g?

(A) It is accurate to 0.1 g and contains 4 significant figures.
(B) It is accurate to 0.01 g and contains 3 significant figures.
(C) It is accurate to 0.001 g and contains 2 significant figures.
(D) It is accurate to 0.0001 g and contains 1 significant figure.

335. In the periodic table of elements, which are the periods?

(A) The vertical columns
(B) The horizontal rows
(C) The left hand groups
(D) The right hand groups

336. How many neutrons are in an atom of carbon-12?

(A) 2
(B) 4
(C) 6
(D) 24

337. What is the correct electron configuration for magnesium?

(A) $1s^22s^2$
(B) $1s^22s^22p^6$
(C) $1s^22s^22p^63s^2$
(D) $1s^22s^22p^63s^23p^1$

338. What is the molarity of a solution containing 0.45 moles of NaCl in 4 liters?

(A) 0.11 M NaCl
(B) 0.45 M NaCl
(C) 1.8 M NaCl
(D) 8.9 M NaCl

339. On the periodic table, what does 12.01 represent in the box for carbon?

(A) The atomic number for carbon
(B) The molarity of carbon
(C) The atomic weight of carbon
(D) The number of electrons in carbon

340. What is a cation?

(A) A positively charged ion
(B) A negatively charged ion
(C) A positively charged covalent bond
(D) A negatively charged covalent bond

341. Which element has the lowest melting point and boiling point of all?

(A) Carbon
(B) Helium
(C) Neon
(D) Oxygen

342. Which solution would change red litmus paper to blue?

(A) NaCl
(B) NaOH
(C) HNO_3
(D) H_2SO_4

343. If 58.5 g of NaCl (1 mole of NaCl) are dissolved in enough water to make 0.500 L of solution, what is the molarity of the solution?

(A) 1.0 M
(B) 2.0 M
(C) 11.7 M
(D) The answer cannot be determined from the information given.

344. What is the correct formula for sodium nitrate?

(A) Na_2NO
(B) Na_3NO
(C) $NaNO_2$
(D) $NaNO_3$

345. Why does fluorine have a higher ionization energy than oxygen?

   (A) Fluorine has a smaller number of neutrons.
   (B) Fluorine has a larger number of neutrons.
   (C) Fluorine has a smaller nuclear charge.
   (D) Fluorine has a larger nuclear charge.

346. Name the reaction shown.

$$8Fe + S_8 \rightarrow 8FeS$$

   (A) Single displacement
   (B) Double displacement
   (C) Synthesis
   (D) Acid-base

347. The energy required to remove the outermost electron from an atom is called _____.

   (A) covalent bonding
   (B) electronegativity
   (C) atomic radius
   (D) ionization energy

348. Which is a triatomic allotrope of oxygen?

   (A) Ozone
   (B) Water
   (C) Acidic oxide
   (D) Carbon dioxide

349. What is the name of the compound $CH_3\text{-}CH_2\text{-}CH_2\text{-}CH_3$?

   (A) Cyclobutane
   (B) Butane
   (C) Butene
   (D) Butyne

350. What is the product of combustion of a hydrocarbon in excess oxygen?

   (A) Carbon dioxide and water
   (B) Naphthalene
   (C) Chlorine and bromine
   (D) Carbonium ions

351. Balance this equation: $Zn + HCl \rightarrow ZnCl_2 + H_2$

    (A) $Zn + 2HCl \rightarrow ZnCl_2 + H_2$
    (B) $Zn + HCl \rightarrow 2ZnCl_2 + H_2$
    (C) $2Zn + HCl \rightarrow 2ZnCl_2 + H_2$
    (D) $Zn + 4HCl \rightarrow ZnCl_2 + H_2$

352. On the periodic table, where are atoms with the largest atomic radius located?

    (A) At the top of their group
    (B) In the middle of their group
    (C) At the bottom of their group
    (D) Along the right hand side

353. Which of these is an organic compound?

    (A) HCl
    (B) NH_3
    (C) CO_2
    (D) CH_4

354. Which compound is represented by this structure?

$$\begin{array}{c} H \quad H \\ H \underset{\underset{H}{|}}{\overset{}{C}} \underset{\underset{H}{|}}{\overset{|}{C}} \underset{\underset{H}{|}}{\overset{}{C}} H \\ H \quad H \quad H \end{array}$$

    (A) Ammonia
    (B) Carbon monoxide
    (C) Hydrogen peroxide
    (D) Propane

355. What is the charge of an alpha ray?

    (A) -1
    (B) $+1$
    (C) $+2$
    (D) No charge

356. What is the correct name of $AgNO_3$?

    (A) Argent nitrous
    (B) Argent oxide
    (C) Silver nitrite
    (D) Silver nitrate

357. What is the oxidation state of the chlorine atom in the compound HCl?

(A) +1
(B) −1
(C) +2
(D) −2

358. $Al(NO_3)_3 + H_2SO_4 \rightarrow Al_2(SO_4)_3 + HNO_3$ is an example of which kind of reaction?

(A) Decomposition reaction
(B) Synthesis reaction
(C) Single replacement reaction
(D) Double replacement reaction

359. B, Si, As, Te, At, Ge, and Sb form a staircase pattern on the right side of the periodic table. How can these elements be classified?

(A) As metals
(B) As semimetals
(C) As nonmetals
(D) As ultrametals

360. If gas A has four times the molar mass of gas B, you would expect it to diffuse through a plug _____.

(A) at half the rate of gas B
(B) at twice the rate of gas B
(C) at a quarter the rate of gas B
(D) at four times the rate of gas B

361. Which element might you encounter in nature in its pure form?

(A) Au
(B) K
(C) Li
(D) B

362. If a neutral sodium atom has one electron removed, what is the result?

(A) A negatively charged Na^- ion with a net charge of +1
(B) A positively charged Na^+ ion with a net charge of −1
(C) A negatively charged Na^- ion with a net charge of −1
(D) A positively charged Na^+ ion with a net charge of +1

363. If you leave a metal rake outside and it rusts, what reaction has taken place?

(A) Double displacement
(B) Acid-base
(C) Combustion
(D) Oxidation-reduction

364. Which material would you expect to have the highest melting point?

(A) Silver
(B) Lead
(C) Iron
(D) Copper

365. How do organic reactions compare to inorganic reactions?

(A) They are slower due to the presence of covalent bonds.
(B) They are slower due to the presence of multiple ions.
(C) They are faster due to the presence of covalent bonds.
(D) They are faster due to the presence of multiple ions.

366. What is the coefficient of O_2 after the following equation is balanced?

$$\_\_CH_4 + \_\_O_2 \rightarrow \_\_CO_2 + \_\_H_2O$$

(A) 1
(B) 2
(C) 3
(D) 4

367. Which element would you expect to be least reactive?

(A) Li
(B) Cr
(C) Nd
(D) Xe

368. Which is a property of an ionic compound?

(A) Low melting point
(B) Poor conductivity
(C) Shared electrons
(D) Crystalline shape

369. What is the mass number of an atom with 24 protons, 24 electrons, and 30 neutrons?

(A) 24
(B) 30
(C) 48
(D) 54

370. What is the correct name of $ZnSO_4$?

(A) Zinc sulfate
(B) Zinc sulfide
(C) Zinc sulfur
(D) Zinc oxide

371. What is the oxidation state of the oxygen atom in the compound NaOH?

(A) −2
(B) −1
(C) 0
(D) +2

372. Which of these intermolecular forces would have the lowest boiling point?

(A) Dipole–dipole interaction
(B) London dispersion force
(C) Keesom interaction
(D) Hydrogen bonding

373. Which two halogens are gases at room temperature?

(A) Iodine and chlorine
(B) Bromine and iodine
(C) Fluorine and bromine
(D) Chlorine and fluorine

374. Which process has the greatest overall effect on solubility?

(A) Straining
(B) Stirring
(C) Pressure
(D) Heating

375. Which substance would be the best conductor of electricity?

(A) Neon
(B) Silicon
(C) Silver
(D) Mercury

376. Why is salt often used on icy roads?

(A) It forms an ionic bond with water.
(B) It remains crystalized at low temperatures.
(C) Its particles lower the freezing point of water.
(D) It does not dissolve below 0 degrees Celsius.

377. When a metallic atom combines with a nonmetallic atom, what typically happens to the metallic atom?

(A) It gains electrons and forms negative ions.
(B) It loses electrons and forms positive ions.
(C) It gains electrons and forms positive ions.
(D) It loses electrons and forms negative ions.

378. Which compound contains a polar covalent bond?

(A) O_2
(B) F_2
(C) Br_2
(D) H_2O

379. AB $\rightarrow$ A + B represents what type of chemical reaction?

(A) Synthesis
(B) Decomposition
(C) Single replacement
(D) Double replacement

380. Among the following elements, which is a nonmetal?

(A) Mercury
(B) Magnesium
(C) Sulfur
(D) Potassium

CHAPTER 7

Anatomy and Physiology

381. In most ectopic pregnancies, where does the embryo implant?

(A) In the uterus
(B) In the pelvic bone
(C) In the vagina
(D) In the fallopian tube

382. What is the primary hormone secreted by the thyroid?

(A) Oxytocin
(B) TSH
(C) Adrenaline
(D) T4

383. Which might you expect to see in a whiplash injury?

(A) Cardiopulmonary problems
(B) Side-to-side spinal curvature
(C) Eventual herniation of discs
(D) Traumatic injury to ligaments

384. Muscle contractions that normally move food along the human digestive system are known as _____.

(A) defecation
(B) osmosis
(C) peristalsis
(D) circulation

385. Which type of nutrient does *not* provide the body with energy?

(A) Vitamin
(B) Carbohydrate
(C) Fat
(D) Protein

386. Where does gas exchange take place in the lungs?

(A) Alveoli
(B) Bronchioles
(C) Trachea
(D) Pleura

387. Which is *not* produced by the pituitary gland?

(A) FSH
(B) TRH
(C) LH
(D) ADH

388. The ribs are _____ to the lungs in the human body.

(A) medial
(B) distal
(C) anterior
(D) deep

389. What is the normal pH of human arterial blood?

(A) 6.8
(B) 7.4
(C) 7.9
(D) 8.2

390. Which part of the brain controls balance and coordination?

(A) Parietal lobe
(B) Hypothalamus
(C) Cerebellum
(D) Occipital lobe

391. Which enzyme functions to break down a specific sugar?

(A) Catalase
(B) Lipase
(C) Protease
(D) Lactase

392. The hypothalamus is part of the _____.

(A) cardiovascular system
(B) endocrine system
(C) respiratory system
(D) lymphatic system

393. Which mineral helps to maintain fluid balance in the body?

(A) Potassium
(B) Cobalt
(C) Chromium
(D) Sulfur

394. What is one function of the pineal gland?

(A) Regulation of sleep
(B) Stimulation of growth
(C) Production of milk
(D) Reduction of inflammation

395. How might vitamin D deficiency present?

(A) As bleeding gums
(B) As swollen extremities
(C) As red patches
(D) As crooked bones

396. How does the lymphatic system work with the circulatory system?

(A) The circulatory system produces red blood cells for the lymphatic system.
(B) Lymph draws excess fluid from the cells and deposits it into the blood vessels.
(C) The heart regulates the production of lymph in the lymph glands.
(D) White cells from the lymphatic system eliminate excess red blood cells.

397. What is the function of parathyroid hormone?

(A) Increase of energy levels
(B) Stimulating cell reproduction
(C) Speeding up metabolism
(D) Activating vitamin D

398. Which is *not* an important electrolyte?

(A) Potassium
(B) Nitrogen
(C) Sodium
(D) Calcium

399. Which is *not* true of the epidermis?

(A) It is composed of several layers.
(B) It contains no blood vessels.
(C) It houses the hair follicles.
(D) It contains melanin pigment.

400. The axial skeletal system contains all of these except the _____.

(A) skull
(B) ribs
(C) breastbone
(D) radius

401. The gall bladder is part of the _____.

(A) endocrine system
(B) urinary system
(C) digestive system
(D) nervous system

402. Which is *not* an example of a nonspecific immune response?

(A) Inflammation
(B) Vasodilation
(C) Releases of histamine.
(D) Production of antibodies

403. Which mineral is important for the formation of red blood cells?

(A) Selenium
(B) Calcium
(C) Magnesium
(D) Copper

404. The dorsal body cavity is _____ to the ventral body cavity.

(A) medial
(B) deep
(C) posterior
(D) anterior

405. Which organ system is primarily responsible for preventing water loss?

(A) The nervous system
(B) The integumentary system
(C) The lymphatic system
(D) The urinary system

406. Which is the only long bone in the human body to lie horizontally?

(A) Clavicle
(B) Humerus
(C) Scapula
(D) Ischium

407. Unlike the cone cells in the eye, the rod cells are responsible for _____.

(A) color vision
(B) depth perception
(C) night vision
(D) eye color

408. A pneumothorax is caused by an unusual buildup of air in the _____.

(A) lungs
(B) pleural cavity
(C) trachea
(D) pulmonary vein

409. Where might a herniated lumbar disc be most likely to create pain?

(A) Along the radial nerve
(B) Within the spinal cord
(C) Along the sciatic nerve
(D) Along the plantar nerves

410. What is the name of the bone in the human thigh?

(A) Ulna
(B) Femur
(C) Radius
(D) Humerus

411. The ovaries are part of the _____.

(A) skeletal system
(B) nervous system
(C) lymphatic system
(D) reproductive system

412. What is another term for the zygomatic bone?

(A) Maxilla
(B) Jawbone
(C) Eye socket
(D) Cheekbone

413. What is urea?

(A) Colorless liquid in urine
(B) End product of protein metabolism
(C) Molecule produced by the kidneys
(D) Fluid stored in the bladder

414. Round muscles called *sphincters* may be found in all of these structures *except* the _____.

(A) anus
(B) iris
(C) esophagus
(D) talus

415. Histology is the study of _____.

(A) blood
(B) cells and tissues
(C) the heart
(D) symptoms

416. The corpus callosum facilitates communication between the ____.

(A) left and right brain
(B) skeletal and neural systems
(C) brain and spinal cord
(D) thalamus and hypothalamus

417. How does the integumentary system work with the nervous system?

(A) The integumentary system removes heat from the neurons in the nervous system.
(B) The nervous system circulates nutrients outward to the integumentary system.
(C) Touch input via the integumentary system sends messages to the nervous system.
(D) Messages from the nervous system affect the color and texture of the skin.

418. When the pulmonary valve and aortic valves are open, where can blood flow?

(A) Between the two ventricles of the heart
(B) From atrium to ventricle within the heart
(C) Between the heart and the rest of the body
(D) Between the atria in the heart

419. Which muscle flexes the forearm at the elbow?

(A) Bicep
(B) Tricep
(C) Deltoid
(D) Flexor carpi ulnaris

420. What are the components of chyle?

(A) Nutrients and erythrocytes
(B) Proteins and electrolytes
(C) Cholesterol and salts
(D) Lymph and fatty acids

421. At which point does bile enter the gastrointestinal tract?

(A) Cecum
(B) Jejunum
(C) Ileum
(D) Duodenum

422. Which is a secondary defense for the body against pathogens?

(A) Tears
(B) Urine
(C) Inflammation
(D) Mucus

423. Which organ system is primarily responsible for storing minerals?

(A) The skeletal system
(B) The endocrine system
(C) The lymphatic system
(D) The cardiovascular system

424. The vena cavae drain blood from the body into the _____.

(A) right atrium
(B) right ventricle
(C) left atrium
(D) left ventricle

425. At which point is an impulse transmitted between neurons?

(A) Synapse
(B) Dendrite
(C) Ganglion
(D) Axon

426. The primary genitalia of a human female would include which of these organs?

(A) Gonads
(B) Testes
(C) Vulva
(D) Uterus

427. Which gland secretes epinephrine?

(A) Pituitary
(B) Pineal
(C) Pancreas
(D) Adrenal

428. Which bone in the foot has no analogous bone in the hand?

(A) Phalanges
(B) Metatarsal
(C) Tarsal
(D) Calcaneus

429. Which is *not* a part of the limbic system?

(A) Olfactory bulb
(B) Medulla oblongata
(C) Amygdala
(D) Hippocampus

430. How does a sagittal section divide the body?

(A) Into right and left regions
(B) Into upper and lower regions
(C) Into front and back regions
(D) Between the dorsal and ventral cavities

431. Which is an anterior feature of the human head?

(A) The nose
(B) The ears
(C) The occipital lobe
(D) The temporal lobe

432. The diaphragm separates the _____ cavities.

(A) abdominal and thoracic
(B) cranial and vertebral
(C) vertebral and pericardial
(D) pelvic and abdominal

433. Enlargement of the thyroid, commonly known as a goiter, might be expected to affect _____.

(A) swallowing
(B) insulin levels
(C) sleep
(D) digestion

434. Which part of the human ear compresses sound waves and passes them to the inner ear?

(A) Eardrum
(B) Cochlea
(C) Stirrup
(D) Pinna

435. How do red blood cells carry oxygen?

(A) They dissolve it in plasma.
(B) They break it down from CO_2.
(C) O_2 molecules replace cell nuclei.
(D) Hemoglobin bonds with O_2 molecules.

436. What does the thyroid require in order to make T4?

(A) Potassium
(B) Iodine
(C) Sodium
(D) Magnesium

437. Where might you find smooth muscle?

(A) In the heart
(B) In the head and neck
(C) In the walls of blood vessels
(D) In the torso and limbs

438. What is the purpose of valves in veins?

(A) To filter impurities
(B) To synchronize flow
(C) To separate veins from arteries
(D) To prevent reverse flow

439. Which of the following are considered normal values for the measure of a person's pulse and blood pressure?

(A) 55 beats per minute and 75 over 60 mm Hg
(B) 72 beats per minute and 120 over 80 mm Hg
(C) 100 beats per minute and 140 over 100 mm Hg
(D) 160 beats per minute and 100 over 70 mm Hg

440. How do humans use their anterior nares?

(A) For inhaling
(B) For tasting
(C) For regulating stress
(D) For directing sound

441. How is pepsin used by the body?

(A) To break down proteins
(B) To break down starches
(C) To emulsify fats and oils
(D) To absorb water and nutrients

442. What are the two main parts of the mammalian skull?

(A) The temporal bone and the occipital bone
(B) The maxilla and the mandible
(C) The mandible and the cranium
(D) The frontal bone and the temporal bone

443. Which tissue connects muscle to bone?

(A) Fasciae
(B) Tendon
(C) Ligament
(D) Cartilage

444. One-third of the protein in the human body is _____.

(A) Collagen
(B) Casein
(C) Keratin
(D) Hemoglobin

445. When does the pancreas secrete the most insulin?

(A) When blood sugar falls
(B) When blood sugar rises
(C) Before food is consumed
(D) After fat is burned

CHAPTER 8

Physics

446. As a batter hits a ball, the force of the ball on the bat is _____ the force of the bat on the ball.

(A) equal to
(B) less than
(C) greater than
(D) the inverse of

447. The quantum theory of light states that light's energy is carried in units called _____.

(A) photoelectrons
(B) photons
(C) waves
(D) corpuscles

448. As an object falls with no air resistance, what happens?

(A) Its velocity increases.
(B) Its acceleration increases.
(C) Its velocity and acceleration increase.
(D) It maintains a constant velocity.

449. Which force represents positive work?

(A) Using the force of friction to stop a rolling golf ball
(B) Using applied force to slow a subway train at a station
(C) Using applied force to hammer a nail into a board
(D) Using tension to string holiday lights from a wire

450. Tuning a radio matches the frequency of an internal electrical circuit to the frequency employed by the radio station. What principle does this illustrate?

(A) Harmonics
(B) Reverberation
(C) Constructive interference
(D) Resonance

451. How might the energy use of an appliance be expressed?

(A) Power = energy × time
(B) Time + energy = power
(C) Energy = power × time
(D) Energy/power = time

452. A force of 12 kg stretches a spring 3 cm. How far will the spring stretch given a force of 30 kg?

(A) 6 cm
(B) 7.5 cm
(C) 9 cm
(D) 10.5 cm

453. A 2,000-kg car runs around a track at 10 m/s with a centripetal acceleration of 4 m/s². What is the radius of the track?

(A) 1,000 m
(B) 400 m
(C) 25 m
(D) 12 m

454. You rub a neutral plastic cup with a cotton ball, giving the cup a positive charge. What is true of the cotton ball?

(A) It has lost electrons.
(B) It has a negative charge.
(C) It has lost neutrons.
(D) It has more protons than electrons.

455. Two objects attract each other with a gravitational force of 12 units. If you double the distance between the objects, what is the new force of attraction between the two?

(A) 3 units
(B) 6 units
(C) 24 units
(D) 48 units

456. What is the purpose of a switch in a circuit?

(A) To reverse the direction of alternating current
(B) To increase the voltage of the battery or cell
(C) To increase the resistance of wires in the circuit
(D) To allow the circuit to open and close

457. When a car is driven for a long time, the pressure of air in the tires increases. This is best explained by which of the following gas laws?

(A) Boyle's Law
(B) Charles's Law
(C) Gay-Lussac's Law
(D) Dalton's Law

458. An ampere is the amount of electric current existing when one _____ flows past a point on a circuit in one second.

(A) volt
(B) ohm
(C) coulomb
(D) watt

459. A hummingbird's wings beat at 25 beats per second. What is the period of the wing beating in seconds?

(A) 0.04 s
(B) 0.25 s
(C) 0.4 s
(D) 4 s

460. What is the kinetic energy of a 500-kg wagon moving at 10 m/s?

(A) 50 J
(B) 250 J
(C) 2.5×10^4 J
(D) 5.0×10^5 J

461. The specific heat capacity of tin is 0.217 J/(g°C). Which of these materials would require about twice as much heat as tin to increase the temperature of a sample by 1°C?

(A) Copper [0.3844 J/(g°C)]
(B) Iron [0.449 J/(g°C)]
(C) Gold [0.1291 J/(g°C)]
(D) Aluminum [0.904 J/(g°C)]

462. An astronaut's mass on Earth is 85 kg. What is his mass on Jupiter, where the force of gravity is about 2.53 times that of gravity on Earth?

(A) 33.6 kg
(B) 85 kg
(C) 87.53 kg
(D) 215.05 kg

463. A baby slides an empty box across the floor. If the baby puts her wooden blocks into the box and continues to slide the box, what happens to the force of kinetic friction between the box and the floor?

(A) It decreases.
(B) It increases.
(C) It remains the same.
(D) It is halved.

464. A car, starting from rest, accelerates at 10 m/s² for 5 seconds. What is the velocity of the car after 5 seconds?

(A) 2 m/s
(B) 5 m/s
(C) 50 m/s
(D) The answer cannot be determined from the information given.

465. A 10-kg object moving at 5 m/s has an impulse acted on it causing the velocity to change to 15 m/s. What was the impulse that was applied to the object?

(A) 10 kg·m/s
(B) 15 kg·m/s
(C) 20 kg·m/s
(D) 100 kg·m/s

466. Which substance's volume would be most affected by temperature change?

(A) Liquid nitrogen
(B) Salt crystals
(C) Hydrogen gas
(D) Iron filings

467. As a batter hits a ball, the acceleration of the bat is _____ the acceleration of the ball.

(A) equal to
(B) less than
(C) greater than
(D) the inverse of

468. What happens when you polarize light?

(A) You absorb most of its electromagnetic radiation.
(B) You reduce the amplitude of the waves.
(C) You separate it into individual colors.
(D) You restrict its vibrations to a single plane.

469. If you double the speed of a moving object, what else doubles?

(A) Its potential energy
(B) Its kinetic energy
(C) Its acceleration
(D) Its momentum

470. Which is true of water?

(A) It is opaque to visible light but transparent to ultraviolet light.
(B) It is opaque to ultraviolet light but transparent to visible light.
(C) It is opaque both to ultraviolet and visible light.
(D) It is transparent both to ultraviolet and visible light.

471. According to Charles's law, when the pressure on a sample of gas is constant, the Kelvin temperature is proportional to the _____.

(A) mass
(B) volume
(C) expansion
(D) compression

472. Longitudinal waves have vibrations that move _____.

(A) at right angles to the direction of the wave
(B) in a circular motion
(C) in the same or opposite direction as the wave
(D) in waves and troughs

473. Which of the following describes a vector quantity?

(A) 5 miles per hour due southwest
(B) 5 miles per hour
(C) 5 miles
(D) None of the above

474. Why are boats more buoyant in salt water than in fresh water?

(A) Salt decreases the mass of the boats.
(B) Salt increases the volume of the water.
(C) Salt affects the density of the boats.
(D) Salt increases the density of the water.

475. How does a lightning rod work?
    (A) It discharges clouds and prevents lightning.
    (B) It dissipates heat energy from lightning into the air.
    (C) It conducts electric current safely to ground.
    (D) It attracts lightning, keeping it away from structures.

476. Two blocks on a frictionless surface are forced apart by a spring. The first block has a mass of 4 kg and moves left at 3 m/s. If the second block has a mass of 6 kg, how fast will it move to the right?
    (A) 2 m/s
    (B) 3 m/s
    (C) 4 m/s
    (D) 6 m/s

477. Why does light refract when it moves from air into a glass window?
    (A) Its intensity is greater in glass than in air.
    (B) Its frequency is higher in air than in glass.
    (C) It travels more slowly in glass than in air.
    (D) Its energy is greater in air than in glass.

478. To calculate average speed, you must know distance and _____.
    (A) vector
    (B) acceleration
    (C) velocity
    (D) time

479. Which names the approximate freezing point of water?
    (A) 0 K
    (B) 100 K
    (C) 273 K
    (D) 373 K

480. Mixing red, blue, and green light in equal amounts leads to which result?
    (A) Cyan light
    (B) White light
    (C) Magenta light
    (D) Black, or the absence of light

481. Which one has the lowest density?
    (A) Water
    (B) Cork
    (C) Aluminum
    (D) Steel

482. Marilyn is driving to a wedding. She drives 4 miles south before realizing that she left the gift at home. She makes a U-turn, returns home to pick up the gift, and sets out again driving south. This time, she drives 1 mile out of her way to pick up a friend. From there, they continue 5 miles more to the wedding. Which of these statements is true about Marilyn's trip?

   (A) The displacement of her trip is 6 miles, and the distance traveled is 6 miles.
   (B) The displacement of her trip is 14 miles, and the distance traveled is 14 miles.
   (C) The displacement of her trip is 8 miles, and the distance traveled is 14 miles.
   (D) The displacement of her trip is 6 miles, and the distance traveled is 14 miles.

483. If the force on an object is doubled, how does its acceleration change?

   (A) It remains the same.
   (B) It is halved.
   (C) It is doubled.
   (D) It is eliminated.

484. Picture a lever with distance from one end to the fulcrum 10 cm and from the other end to the fulcrum 20 cm. If an input force is applied to the end of the lever farther from the fulcrum, what is the mechanical advantage of the lever?

   (A) ½
   (B) 2
   (C) 20
   (D) 200

485. A CD spins in a CD player at a constant rate. There is a speck of dust on the edge of the CD and a second speck halfway in toward the spindle. Which speck has the greater magnitude of acceleration?

   (A) The speck on the edge
   (B) The speck halfway in
   (C) Both have acceleration of zero.
   (D) Both have the same acceleration.

486. The speed of light would be slowest in which substance?

   (A) Air
   (B) Glass
   (C) Water
   (D) The speed of light never changes.

487. What is the function of a transformer?

(A) To reduce the flow of current within a circuit
(B) To inhibit the conduction of an electric charge
(C) To charge one object by bringing it near a charged object
(D) To increase or reduce voltage of an alternating current

488. Jack stands in front of a plane mirror. If he is 2.5 feet away from the mirror, how far away from Jack is his image?

(A) 2.5 feet
(B) 3 feet
(C) 4.5 feet
(D) 5 feet

489. Ocean waves build during a storm until there is a vertical distance from high point to low of 6 meters and a horizontal distance of 9 meters between adjacent crests. The waves hit the shore every 5 seconds. What is the speed of the waves?

(A) 1.2 m/s
(B) 1.8 m/s
(C) 2.0 m/s
(D) 2.4 m/s

490. If a 5.5 kg ball is moving at 4.5 m/s, what is its momentum?

(A) 10 kg·m/s
(B) 16.2 km/h
(C) 24.75 kg·m/s
(D) There is not enough information to calculate momentum.

491. When is the force on an electron moving in a magnetic field greatest?

(A) When its direction is opposite to that of the magnetic field
(B) When its direction is identical to that of the magnetic field
(C) When its direction is perpendicular to that of the magnetic field
(D) The force is always constant.

492. Heat energy uses only conduction to travel through _____.

(A) gases
(B) liquids
(C) solids
(D) solids and liquids

493. A 1,000-kg car drives at 10 m/s around a circle with a radius of 50 m. What is the centripetal acceleration of the car?

(A) 2 m/s^2
(B) 4 m/s^2
(C) 5 m/s^2
(D) 10 m/s^2

494. A 3-volt flashlight uses a bulb with 60-ohm resistance. What current flows through the flashlight?

(A) 0.05 amp
(B) 0.5 amp
(C) 1.8 amp
(D) 18 amp

495. A balloon with a charge of 5 μC is placed 25 cm from another balloon with the same charge. What is the magnitude of the resulting repulsive force?

(A) 0.18 N
(B) 1.8 N
(C) 10^{-3} N
(D) 5 × 10^{-3} N

496. If a radioactive substance has a half-life of 10 years, what fraction of the substance will remain after 30 years?

(A) One-half
(B) One-third
(C) One-quarter
(D) One-eighth

497. A 1.0-kg block on a table is given a push so that it slides along the table. If the block is accelerated at 6 m/s^2, what was the force applied to the block?

(A) 0 N
(B) 3 N
(C) 6 N
(D) The answer cannot be determined from the information given.

498. A 60-watt lightbulb is powered by a 110-volt power source. What is the current being drawn?

(A) 0.55 amperes
(B) 1.83 amperes
(C) 50 amperes
(D) 6,600 amperes

499. A wave moves through its medium at 20 m/s with a wavelength of 4 m. What is the frequency of the wave?

(A) 5 s^{-1}

(B) 16 s^{-1}

(C) 24 s^{-1}

(D) 80 s^{-1}

500. A candle viewed in a plane mirror will be _____.

(A) inverted and reduced

(B) inverted and enlarged

(C) upright and reduced

(D) upright and equal in size

ANSWER KEY

Chapter 1: Reading Comprehension

1. **(A)** Skim the passage to identify the detail that does not appear. The sports in choice A are never mentioned, so you do not even need to look at the other choices.

2. **(B)** Substitute the choices in place of the vocabulary word. Only *reduced* (B) fits the context.

3. **(A)** Find the summary that best fits the overall substance of the passage. Some choices may be too specific, as B is, or too subjective, as choice D is.

4. **(D)** This passage is primarily informational, providing facts and data about the topic.

5. **(C)** Choices A, B, and D relate directly to information given in the passage. Choice C, on the other hand, is never even hinted at by the author, who speaks of sports-related concussions but does not compare them to other types of concussions.

6. **(A)** Ask yourself, "How does the author feel about drunkorexia? How does she make me feel about it?" The author's word choice evinces a feeling of dismay or concern.

7. **(B)** No one can abstain completely from food—no one can go without it.

8. **(D)** Choices A and B appear in paragraph 1, and choice C appears in paragraph 2. No mention is made of medical cures for this disorder.

9. **(A)** The answer would be choice B, to persuade, if the author were requesting an action or change in beliefs from the reader. Since the author is simply presenting facts and information, the better choice is A.

10. **(A)** The main idea is the idea that applies to the passage as a whole.

11. **(B)** Although choice A is close, the word *compel* means "to force," so a compelling argument is one that forces the listener to a conclusion.

12. **(A)** There is much information here, too, but the author's main reason for writing is to encourage the reader to understand the importance of sun exposure. The first and last sentences in the passage help to clarify this purpose.

13. **(B)** How does the author feel about the topic of sun exposure? The only reasonable answer is choice B, *confident*. Again, the first and last sentences in the passage clarify this tone.

14. **(C)** Choice C is the only one that sticks to the premise of the passage without focusing too closely on one detail or moving beyond the scope of the essay.

15. (B) Although all of the choices are verbs and thus fit the construction of the sentence, only *keep* makes sense in context. If farmers can keep their land, they can continue to provide your region with open space.

16. (D) The entire essay touts the value of buying locally in an effort to convince the reader that it is a good idea.

17. (A) This summary covers the main idea of the passage, which deals with the benefits of eating locally. The other choices cover only small snippets of the passage as a whole.

18. (B) The other choices may be proved or checked, but choice B is the author's opinion—even though it may be the opinion of many other people as well.

19. (A) Choices B, C, and D are never hinted at by the author, but choice A may be inferred from the description of eating foods in their season, "meaning that we eat them at the peak of flavor and ripeness."

20. (A) The author's attitude toward yoga seems to be positive and sincere. *Earnest* (A) would be a good description of this tone.

21. (C) This question is all about context. The passage refers to the tolerance of pain, making choices A, B, and D illogical.

22. (D) Although statement D may be true, it is not a detail in the passage. Choices A and B are found in paragraph 3, and choice C is in paragraph 4.

23. (A) Although this passage is partly informative, that is not a choice here. The author does present the opinion that everyone should try yoga, making this a persuasive essay.

24. (C) Choice A is not hinted at by the passage. Choice B is a stretch—the author never claims that having red skin means a child must have hypothermia. Choice D is not a claim the author makes. The only logical response is choice C, which is supported by the information in paragraph 2.

25. (D) In general, the author is warning parents of infants about the signs and dangers of hypothermia in their children.

26. (B) All of the other choices are mentioned in the passage.

27. (C) If in doubt, plug the answer choices into the sentence in place of *suffice*.

28. (A) Although the author says that infants do not shiver, she never implies that it is a learned response. The other choices derive from facts in the passage.

29. (C) The passage describes a single experiment that tends to belie choice D but does not nearly lead to the conclusions in choices A or B. The best choice is C—one study cannot be considered conclusive.

30. (B) Substituting the choices for *touted* in the first sentence should make it clear that choice B is best.

31. (B) Think about the author's overall attitude toward aromatherapy. The author does not dismiss it entirely, but she does raise questions about its efficacy. The best choice is B— she is uncertain about the topic.

32. (C) Choices A and D are in paragraph 1, and choice B is in paragraph 2. Choice C is never mentioned.

33. (A) The point of EHRs is that they are unified—they are not piecemeal notes about a patient but rather an extended, integrated series of records.

34. (C) The passage as a whole is about EHRs and how and why they are used, making choice C the best overall answer. The other answers cover only small portions of the passage.

35. (D) Whether something is costly or difficult depends on the eyes of the beholder, making this statement an opinion rather than a fact.

36. (B) The first sentence of paragraph 2 states: "One goal of electronic health records (EHRs) is to produce one seamless record for each patient that follows that patient around the health care system." This has nothing to do with transportation (choice A). The new system might still require multiple doctors, making choice C incorrect, and choice D is too much of a departure from what is being said. The sentence implies that now a patient will have a single record, no matter where that patient goes, implying that before EHRs, the patient might have had many records.

37. (B) The passage never mentions how many hospitals and doctor's offices currently use EHRs. Choice A appears in paragraph 2, and choices C and D appear in paragraph 4.

38. (B) Choices A and C are details from the passage. Choice D could be a main idea of a different passage; this one never deals with the cost of dementia to families. The best choice is B.

39. (D) The onset of dementia is its beginning, or commencement.

40. (C) The author is not trying to get the reader to do or believe anything (choice A); he is merely giving information (choice C).

41. (D) Referring to dementia as "heartbreaking" indicates a sympathetic tone.

42. (B) The summary must include all of the main focuses of the passage, and in this case, only choice B fulfills that objective.

43. (A) The passage is mostly informational, presenting facts about a new study.

44. (B) Print ads were not banned as a result of the Public Health Cigarette Smoking Act. The other changes are mentioned in paragraph 2.

45. (D) The ads urge "moderation" in drinking, meaning that they urge people to moderate their consumption, or practice self-restraint.

46. (B) The study, which is the focus of the passage, showed that young people were more likely to drink certain brands because they saw the brands on television.

47. (A) Although beer advertising is specifically mentioned, you cannot infer that other alcohol advertising does not have a similar effect. The other choices are implied by statements in the passage.

48. (C) *Staphylococcus aureus* is ubiquitous in hospitals—it is found everywhere.

49. (D) Choice A is illogical, choice B is close but does not cover all of the information in the passage, and choice C is never suggested. The best overall statement about the passage is D.

50. (C) A statement of fact can be proved or checked. A statement of opinion is what someone thinks or believes. In this case, statements A, B, and D could be proved scientifically, but statement C is simply someone's belief.

51. (D) If a statement cannot be inferred by the reader, either there is not enough information to draw conclusions about it, or the passage contradicts the inference. The passage implies that MRSA is transmitted primarily by skin-to-skin contact—it is described as a "skin infection," and while using someone's razor might put you at risk, buying used clothing that has been washed is unlikely to be hazardous.

52. (D) The symptoms are described in paragraph 4.

53. (C) Although most of the passage is alarming if not alarmist, the final paragraph suggests that it would be difficult for Ebola to spread as a pandemic, which is mildly reassuring.

54. (A) This is the best conclusion to draw based on the evidence in the passage. Choice B is belied by the fact that the virus is hard to spread, and choices C and D are not implied by the author at all.

55. (B) A fact may be proved or checked, and the speed with which Ebola works is something that might be tested and proved. The other statements are not provable.

56. (D) The passage is not about an ancient disease (choice A) or about a disease that has migrated (choice B). The search for a cure is never mentioned (choice C).

57. (D) The author does not conclude choice A, and the passage does not deal with choice B. Only one paragraph deals with the topic in choice C. The passage is mostly about the pros and cons of barefoot running, making D the best choice.

58. (D) Read the word in context: "There is little consensus when it comes to the safety and effectiveness of barefoot running." The author means that people do not agree on the safety and effectiveness; there is no unanimous opinion about it.

59. (D) All of the other choices have some support in the passage. Although modern running shoes have only been around for 50 years, there is no indication that people ran barefoot before that time.

60. (A) You can test the cost of running shoes (choice B), the hardness of roads and paths (choice C) and even the springiness of the arch (choice D). Whether running barefoot is natural and advantageous remains an opinion (choice A).

61. (A) This is a reasonable restatement of the central idea of the passage.

62. (D) The description of forensic nurses who work with the accused has them working in correction facilities, implying that they step in after someone has been sentenced to jail or prison.

63. (A) Test the choices in place of *pursue* in the sentence. When you pursue a specialization, you take it up or engage in it.

64. (C) Although it is possible that a legal nurse consultant might work on such cases, this is not one of the types of cases mentioned in paragraph 4.

65. (A) The passage is informative and impartial, or neutral.

Chapter 2: Vocabulary and General Knowledge

66. (A) The fact that he generates several studies is a clue to the meaning of *prolific,* which refers to someone who is abundantly creative and productive.

67. (D) The word is from the Latin *vacuus,* meaning "empty," and is related to *vacuum,* as in empty space.

68. (B) To be *circumspect* is to be cautious, or guarded. A nurse who is circumspect with patient records is careful not to let the information get out.

69. (B) Sometimes spelled *staunch,* this word means "to bring to a stop," especially when referring to the flow of blood or other bodily fluids.

70. (A) *Ostracize* is from a Greek word meaning "banish" or "exile." If you ostracize someone, you exclude him or her from your social group.

71. (A) *Indigent* translates literally as "in need."

72. (B) A *nit* is the egg or young of a louse.

73. (A) To *augment* something is to make it greater or to add to it.

74. (D) *Quarantine* comes from the word for "forty." It originally referred to the period of 40 days that a ship was detained in port if it was thought to harbor infectious diseases. Today quarantine is used to separate very contagious patients from the general population.

75. (C) You might give an *emetic* to a victim of poisoning.

76. (D) A *panacea* is literally a cure-all—a remedy for all illness.

77. (C) *Evisceration* has to do with removal of the viscera, the internal organs—or removal of their contents.

78. (B) *Flux* has a variety of meanings, all related to flowing or outflow. In medical terms it often refers to a discharge from the bowels.

79. (C) *Regulations* are used to regulate conduct in a business or government.

80. (C) The word is related to *quarrel* and comes from a Latin word meaning "to complain."

81. (A) *Pernicious*, as in *pernicious anemia*, means "causing great injury."

82. (C) If you are *accountable*, you can account for your actions.

83. (B) *Tendere* means "to stretch," as in *extend*. *Dis* means "apart," as in *distant*.

84. (C) Something that is fluid (choice A) is liquid. Something that is molten (choice B) is hot and melted. Something that is malleable (choice D) is flexible. Only choice C is a synonym for *viscous*.

85. (D) If people are "in collusion," they are conspiring together for the purpose of fraud or crime.

86. (C) Something that is *obsolete* has either gone out of style or been discarded over time. This would not mean that the theory was never true (choice D), simply that it has been revised or replaced.

87. (D) The River Lethe is the river of forgetfulness in Greek mythology. Someone who is *lethargic* is unusually drowsy, forgetful, and dull.

88. (B) An *onus* is a load or a responsibility, so a task that is *onerous* is one that feels like a burden.

89. (D) *Altruism* is the unselfish concern for others. Someone who is *altruistic* gives unselfishly.

90. (B) *Trepidation* comes from a Latin word meaning "to tremble." If students are observing with trepidation, they are uneasy or have misgivings.

91. (A) *Precepts* may be commandments or rules for moral conduct, or they may simply be written directions or guidelines.

92. (D) *Truculence* is fierceness, and is often used to describe speech or writing.

93. **(B)** The best synonym for *counseling* is *advising*.

94. **(A)** The gingival *margin* is the edge of the gums.

95. **(A)** To be *sallow* is to have a sickly, yellowish hue.

96. **(C)** If the record is *exemplary*, it serves as an example, or model. In other words, it is outstanding and praiseworthy.

97. **(C)** Like a nebula cloud of interstellar gas, something that is *nebulous* is cloudy, hazy, or vague.

98. **(A)** A lynx (choice B) is a wildcat; the pharynx (choice C) is part of the alimentary canal, and a phalanx (choice D) may be a bone in the fingers or toes.

99. **(A)** *Contour* means "to go around" and refers to the outline of an object.

100. **(C)** To be *incorrigible* is to be uncorrectable. It is often used to describe the behavior of rambunctious young children.

101. **(A)** *Deteriorate* is literally "to make or become worse." A patient whose condition deteriorates may fail to eat or drink (choice D), but that is a side effect of the overall deterioration, not a definition of the word.

102. **(C)** A precipice is a steep cliff; something that precipitates falls steeply or rushes rapidly, as rain or sleet might do. Something that is *precipitous* is steep or fast-moving.

103. **(A)** If you are predisposed to a condition, you are receptive or susceptible to it ahead of time.

104. **(B)** Something that is *soporific* causes sleepiness. It might be anything from a drug to a dull movie.

105. **(A)** *Disseminate* literally means "to scatter seeds." If you disseminate information, you make it public, or broadcast it.

106. **(C)** *Assiduous* comes from the same root as *assist*. If you are assiduous, you are extremely helpful—you work hard and are industrious.

107. **(D)** To *instigate* an action is to stimulate or incite it, or to activate others.

108. **(C)** If the action is *inhibited*, it is held back, or hindered.

109. **(D)** The symptom may be disfiguring (choice B) or painful (choice C), but it is definitely made worse (choice D) or intensified.

110. **(A)** A *critique* may be positive (choice C) or negative (choices B and D), but it is always some form of assessment or appraisal (choice A).

111. (A) If you are *contrite,* you repent your actions—you regret them and feel sorry for what you have done.

112. (D) Someone who is *guileless* is without guile, or slyness. Such a person is very frank and straightforward.

113. (B) To be redundant is literally to flow over, so a *redundancy* is a surplus or an overflow.

114. (B) *Atrophy* is a wasting away, as may happen to muscles when they go unused for a period of hospitalization. An atrophied body part might look withered, or shrunken and weakened.

115. (C) *Anterior* is the opposite of *posterior*; something that is anterior is near the front.

116. (B) Although *gravid* comes from the same root as *grave* (choice A), it refers to the heaviness of pregnancy, not to seriousness.

117. (B) A wall might be *riddled* with bullet holes; an essay might be *riddled* with errors. Either meaning has to do with being affected throughout.

118. (A) You may have heard the legal term *mitigating circumstances*. Whether it is a crime or symptoms that are mitigated, the meaning has to do with their becoming less severe or less critical.

119. (C) *Banal* used to describe an everyday object owned by a serf. Nowadays, it is used to refer to language or ideas that are dull and hackneyed because they are overused and ordinary.

120. (B) To ramify is to spread out into branches or offshoots. *Ramifications* are offshoots or effects of an action, or that action's consequences.

121. (D) *Respite* has two common meanings: a delay or postponement, or an interval of relief and rest. In the health profession, a respite worker is one who takes over from time to time from a caregiver.

122. (C) Something that is *asymmetric* is not symmetrical; it is irregular, or uneven.

123. (C) *Counterfeit* literally translates as "to make in opposition." A counterfeit watch is fake.

124. (A) *Effectiveness* and *efficacy* stem from the same root; both mean "the power to produce intended results."

125. (C) Think about words with similar parts, such as *rehabilitate*. In this case, the *de-* is a negative prefix. A debilitating disease is one that weakens or incapacitates the patient.

126. (D) An *adroit* surgeon may be admired, scholarly, and sophisticated, but the fact that she is adroit specifically means that she is skillful.

127. (B) *Torrid* means "hot" (choice C), but *torpid* means "inactive," or "sluggish."

128. (D) To *contravene* is literally "to come against." If you contravene orders, you go against them, or disregard them.

129. (B) In four-legged creatures, the *caudal* part is nearest the tail. In humans, it is at the base of the body, toward the feet.

130. (B) The prefix *a-* means "not," so something that is *aseptic* is not septic, or not infected or diseased.

Chapter 3: Grammar

131. (B) The verb form that works in the sentence is *consuming*.

132. (B) Placing a semicolon between *England* and *he* correctly separates the clauses in the sentence.

133. (C) Of the four choices, choices B, C, and D are syntactically correct, but only *therefore* makes sense in context. Since few students were able to complete the assignment, the professor gave them extra time. *Therefore* indicates this cause-and-effect relationship.

134. (D) *Nurses'* is a plural possessive noun that must be replaced by a plural possessive pronoun.

135. (A) The boy must be moving *stealthily*; *stealthy* is an adjective, not an adverb.

136. (D) Who was watching the TV news? Was it the criminals, or was it the person speaking? Only choice D places the modifying phrase next to the word it modifies.

137. (A) *Mayor* is spelled with an *o*.

138. (C) *Must of* (choice A) is never correct; the construction should be *must have*.

139. (D) *Seizure* does not follow the "*I* before *E* except after *C*" rule you may remember from childhood. It is from the Old French word *seizir*.

140. (A) Jake was not accompanied by toast, his eggs and grits were. The phrase would be better placed at the end of the sentence.

141. (B) Choice C would be correct if it were *having finished*, but of the choices given, only choice B works grammatically. Say the sentence aloud to check your answer.

142. (D) *Don't* is a contraction that requires an apostrophe.

143. (B) A proscription is a ban or prohibition; a prescription is something a physician would write for a pharmacist to fill.

144. (B) The sentence is missing its end punctuation. Since it is a question, it needs a question mark.

145. (A) A related word is *disciple*.

146. (D) Choice A makes it seem as though the film has to do with a session with the hospital administrator. Choices B and C are in the passive voice. Only choice D is both active and clear.

147. (C) To ensure that the *c* is pronounced correctly, the *e* must be part of *noticeable*.

148. (D) In questions like this one, try to find the phrase that, if moved around, would improve the sentence. In this case, *Standing with the refrigerator door open* should really begin the sentence. If it did, all phrases would appear properly next to the nouns that they modify.

149. (A) You consult *with* people, not from, by, or in them.

150. (B) Read the choices aloud if you are in doubt. The only one that contains phrases in logical order is choice B.

151. (A) This is a frequently misspelled word that must simply be memorized.

152. (C) *Nugatory* does not mean "negative"; it means "insignificant." You cannot have insignificant significant effects.

153. (A) The committee is working as a unit to produce a single report, so *its*, meaning "belonging to it," is an appropriate pronoun. If the committee worked as separate individuals to prepare a variety of reports, the pronoun might be *their* (choice B).

154. (B) Two independent clauses separated by *and* require a comma before the conjunction.

155. (D) The fact that the word means "not ceasing" may help with its spelling.

156. (C) *Whom* is an object pronoun that correctly may be used as the object of a preposition, as in *to whom*.

157. (C) A colon may be used to precede a list; in this case, the three choices for wall coverings.

158. (D) *Taken* is the verb form that goes with *having*.

159. (A) Ms. Schuster is the one tapping the beat, so the modifying phrase should be as close as possible to her name.

160. (B) The subject of the sentence is *one*, so the verb should be singular.

161. (D) *Professor, profession,* and *professional* all have one *f* and two *s*'s.

162. (A) When the second independent clause in a sentence begins with a conjunctive adverb (*nevertheless, however, similarly*), a comma must follow that adverb. The correct sentence would read: "I did not entirely understand his instructions; nevertheless, I attempted to hook up the computer on my own."

163. (C) The verb might also be *have,* but that is not an option here.

164. (D) Quotation marks are not necessary, because there is no direct quote in the sentence. A comma must separate the dependent and independent clauses.

165. (B) *Progeny* means "children" and may be used in the plural as in this sentence. *Prodigy* means "a young virtuoso or genius" and is singular.

166. (C) *Then* is an adverb meaning "at that time." The word required here is *than,* a conjunction.

167. (C) A comma should come between the introductory clause (*Although we had met earlier*) and the rest of the sentence.

168. (D) Thinking about laboring in the laboratory may help you remember how to spell this word.

169. (B) The sentence is composed of two independent clauses, and the second clause begins with an adverb. A semicolon must separate the clauses, with a comma following the adverb.

170. (C) Reading the choices aloud may help you determine which choice has a logical order of phrases and clauses. The least convoluted sentence is choice C.

171. (B) The word that means "at a previous time" is *formerly,* not *formally.*

172. (A) The correct pronoun must be a subject pronoun. Only choice A is a subject pronoun.

173. (A) Choice D would be correct if *reminds* were *reminding* or *that reminded.* Reading choices aloud can help you find the correct response.

174. (D) If choice A were *sit,* it would be correct. The correct verb is *lie,* meaning "to rest or recline," not *lay* (choice C), meaning "to put something down."

175. (A) Although it derives from the same root as *machine* (choice D), the word *machine* is not in *mechanical.*

176. (B) Only the introductory clause requires a comma to separate it from the independent clause it precedes.

177. (B) If something is situated in the middle of two other things, it is *between* them.

178. (A) The phrase is *sphere of influence*, meaning "range of authority or impact."

179. (A) The prefix *ir-* is added here to the adjective *relevant.*

180. (B) Choice B correctly separates the independent clauses with a semicolon.

181. (D) The action takes place in the future—the time between now and when the semester ends. Therefore, the verb must be in the future tense.

182. (A) The foxes are not ingenuous, meaning "naive." They are ingenious, meaning "clever."

183. (C) You may choose *between* two things or *among* three or more.

184. (B) Jeremiah could seem enthusiastic, an adjective, but he could not seem enthusiastically, an adverb. He could cheer enthusiastically, but *seem* is a linking verb that links Jeremiah to an adjective that describes him.

185. (A) Pronouns that are the objects of a preposition (*to*) must be object pronouns, and naming oneself last is a convention of standard English.

186. (A) The pronoun must replace *Kendra's*, so it must be a third-person, feminine, possessive pronoun. *Hers* (choice D) would only be correct if the pronoun were not modifying a noun (*books*).

187. (B) The root word is *prefer*, which has one *f* and one *r*. The suffix must simply be memorized.

188. (D) Placing a semicolon between the clause *Follow my lead* and the rest of the sentence would make this sentence correct.

189. (B) In this type of question, you must make sure that the tense of verbs remains consistent. Because *was* is past tense, the correct answer contains another past-tense verb, *raised.*

190. (C) The construction of the sentence calls for an adverb, *initially*, not an adjective, *initial.*

191. (D) In choice A, the window seems to have replaced its own glass. Choice B is passive—no one is replacing the glass. Choice C is awkward. Choice D correctly tells who replaced the glass, avoiding the passive voice.

192. (C) The correct superlative adjective is *most inspirational.* The sentence compares the speaker to all other speakers, making choice B incorrect.

193. (D) *Debonair* means "fashionable and confident." It comes from the Old French phrase *de bon aire*, meaning "of good disposition."

194. (B) When used as an adjective, which it usually is, *first-class* requires a hyphen.

195. (D) Quotation marks must enclose the entire question, including its punctuation, and the pronoun identifying the speaker should not be capitalized.

Chapter 4: Basic Math Skills

196. (11) Beatrice received $1.75 in change from her $10 bill, so she spent $10 − $1.75, or $8.25. To find how many dishes she bought at $.75 apiece, divide $.75 into the amount she spent: $8.25 ÷ $.75 = 11.

197. (C) First, find the lowest common denominator, which in this case is 3 × 4 × 5, or 60:

$\frac{1}{3}$	$\frac{1}{4}$	$\frac{1}{5}$
↓	↓	↓
$\frac{20}{60}$	$\frac{15}{60}$	$\frac{12}{60}$

Add the numerators: 20 + 15 + 12 = 47, so the sum is 47/60.

198. (D) Even if you do not know the formula, you should know that 32°F = 0°C, so a few degrees up the Fahrenheit scale should equate to a few degrees up the Celsius scale.

199. (B) You can solve this by creating a function table:

Week	1	2	3	4	5	6	7	8	9	10	11	12
Miles	4	6	8	10	12	14	16	18	20	22	24	26

200. (B) Think: $0.80x = 24$. Solve: $x = 24 ÷ 0.80$. The answer is 30.

201. (D) Set this up as a proportion: $\frac{2}{5} = x/145$. You may cross-multiply to solve:

$$2 \times 145 = 5x$$

$$290 = 5x$$

$$x = \frac{290}{5}$$

$$x = 58$$

202. (A) First, determine how much Stu spent for the cups: $.25 × 6 = $1.50. Then find out what he spent for the plates: $.75 × 6 = $4.50. Add those sums: $1.50 + $4.50 = $6.00. Finally, subtract that total from $10.00: $10.00 − $6.00 = $4.00.

203. (D) 3.08 equals $3\frac{8}{100}$, which is $3\frac{2}{25}$ in lowest terms.

204. (A) Rosie put half of her earnings into savings, so $239.98 ÷ 2 = $119.99. Out of that, she spent $65, so $119.99 − $65 = $54.99.

205. (A) 120% of a number is the original number (100%) plus 20% of that number.

206. (B) Find the lowest common denominator, which in this case is 12.

½	¼	⅙
↓	↓	↓
⁶⁄₁₂	³⁄₁₂	²⁄₁₂

Then, add the numerators: 6 + 3 + 2 = 11.

207. (B) Multiplying two numbers with two digits to the right of the decimal point should result in a product with four digits to the right of the decimal point. However, in this case, the final digit, 0, is dropped off.

208. (25) You are asked to find the percentage of SUVs out of the whole number of vehicles, so first you must add to find the number of vehicles in all: 7 + 7 + 28 + 14 = 56. 14 is ¼ of 56, so the percentage of SUVs is 25%.

209. (D) There are 5 stars in our Arabic or decimal system of numbers. In the binary system, that would be 101, where 1 = 1 four, 0 = 0 twos, and 1 = 1 one.

210. (C) You know that 4 × 5 = 20, so this is just a matter of finding where to place the decimal point. The answer should have three places to the right of the decimal point, so 0.4 × 0.05 = 0.020, or 0.02.

211. (D) M = 1,000. CM = 900. XX = 20. IX = 9.

212. (C) If 6 apples cost $5.70, the unit cost, or price of 1 apple, was $5.70 ÷ 6, or $.95. Dividing that into Sarah's expenditure gets you the number of apples she purchased: $3.80 ÷ $.95 = 4.

213. (A) You may find 15% of 220 and subtract, or you may find 85% of 220. 0.85 × 220 = 187.

214. (16) There are 4 quarts in a gallon, so in 4 gallons, there are 16 quarts.

215. (D) Percentages are fractions of 100, so you must multiply numerator and denominator by 20 to find the percent.

216. (C) If 1 mile approximately equals 1.6 kilometers, 12 miles approximately equals 1.6 × 12, or 19.2 kilometers.

217. (1165) Reading from left to right, M = 1,000, C = 100, L = 50, and XV = 15, making the date 1165.

218. (C) Military time uses a 24-hour clock where 1200 is noon, 1800 is 6:00 P.M., and 2400 is midnight.

219. (C) If the train travels 300 miles in 2½ hours, it travels 300 ÷ 2.5, or 120 miles in 1 hour. Multiplying that by 3 gets you the distance covered in 3 hours: 120 × 3 = 360.

220. (C) Multiply $.35 by 6 to find how much Kate paid: $.35 × 6 = $2.10. Subtracting that from $5 gives you $2.90.

221. (D) Because 1 meter = around 3.28 feet, 6 meters = 3.28 × 6 feet, or 19.68 feet.

222. (A) A percentage is equivalent to a fraction with a denominator of 100. Think $^{25}/_{80} = x/100$. Cross-multiply to get the answer:

$$2,500 = 80x$$

$$x = 31.25$$

223. (D) If 10 pencils are divided between 2 students, each student gets 5 pencils. For 20 students, you need 20 × 5, or 100 pencils.

224. (C) If you line up the decimal points correctly, this should be an easy subtraction. Alternatively, begin with an estimate: 1.1 − 0.9 = 0.2, so you know the answer is either choice C or choice D.

225. (C) 48% = $^{48}/_{100}$. Divide the numerator and denominator by their greatest common factor, 4, to get $^{12}/_{25}$.

226. (B) The actual population must be an equivalent ratio to 1:12. In the case of choice B, (1 × 85):(12 × 85) = 85:1,020.

227. (C) Express the mixed numbers as improper fractions, and multiply the first by the reciprocal of the second.

$4^5/_8$	$1½$	$^{37}/_8 × ^2/_3$
↓	↓	↓
$^{37}/_8$	$^3/_2$	$^{74}/_{24}$

Now reduce to lowest terms and express the answer as a mixed number. $^{74}/_{24} = ^{37}/_{12} = 3^1/_{12}$.

228. (C) Think: Bai Lin uses 10% + 30% of some unknown total, x, on savings and living expenses. She uses 40%, so $1,545 must represent 60% of that unknown total. Now you have enough information to set up an equation:

$$60\% \text{ of } x = \$1,545$$

$$0.60x = \$1,545$$

$$\$1,545 \div 0.60 = x$$

$$x = \$2,575$$

229. (D) One kilogram equals about 2.2 pounds, so 15 kilograms equals about 33 pounds.

230. (C) The total number of kittens is 3 + 4 + 1 = 8. Since there are 3 black kittens, the litter is ⅜ black, or 37.5% black.

231. (A) First find the lowest common denominator, 35:

$$\frac{4}{7} \qquad\qquad \frac{1}{5}$$

$$\downarrow \qquad\qquad \downarrow$$

$$\frac{20}{35} \qquad\qquad \frac{7}{35}$$

20 – 7 = 13. The fraction ¹³⁄₃₅ is already in lowest terms.

232. (B) Think: 92 ÷ 11 is around 8. 8 × 11 = 88. 92 – 88 = 4, so the remainder is 4.

233. (D) If you know that there are 52 weeks in a year, this should be fairly simple. He runs 4 + 3 miles a week, so he runs 7 × 52 miles a year, or 364 miles.

234. (A) Change the percent to a decimal and multiply to solve: 0.15 × 95 = 14.25.

235. (D) You may use cross-multiplication if you like:

$$4 \times x = 6 \times 120$$

$$4x = 720$$

$$x = 720 \div 4$$

$$x = 180$$

236. (B) If Alex triples the recipe, he now needs 3 pints of cream. There are 2 pints in a quart, so he needs 1 quart plus 1 pint.

237. (D) The actual number must have the same ratio as the original 2:13. Another way of thinking about this is that the numbers must be equivalent fractions, or $\frac{2}{13}$ must equal the answer. The only correct response is choice D: $\frac{2}{13} \times \frac{32}{32} = \frac{64}{416}$.

238. (C) 100% of 84 is 84, so 126 must be 100% + 42, or 150%.

239. (2) Figure out how much Leon spent:

$$3 \times \$.85 = \$2.55$$

$$2 \times \$1.49 = \$2.98$$

$$\$2.55 + \$2.98 + \$1.75 = \$7.28$$

Leon gave the cashier $8, so he must have received $8 − $7.28, or $.72 in change. He could only have received 2 quarters in his change.

240. (B) Since you are multiplying a number with two digits after the decimal point by a number with one digit after the decimal point, the answer should have three digits after the decimal point.

241. (D) The formula is $C \times \frac{9}{5} + 32 = F$: $22 \times \frac{9}{5} + 32 = 71.6$.

242. (B) You can find the answer by setting up the easier of the two possible proportions: $\frac{1}{50} = 10/x$, so $x = 500$ cm. Since 500 cm = 5 m, you should be able to rule out all of the choices but choice B.

243. (D) $1\frac{2}{3}$ is equivalent to the improper fraction $\frac{5}{3}$. $3\frac{1}{2}$ is equivalent to the improper fraction $\frac{7}{2}$. Multiply the numerators: $5 \times 7 = 35$. Multiply the denominators: $3 \times 2 = 6$. $\frac{35}{6} = 5\frac{5}{6}$.

244. (C) The question asks you to find "What percent of 22 is 3.75?" To find that, simply divide 3.75 by 22. $3.75 \div 22 = 0.17045\ldots$, so the answer is choice C.

245. (250) One centimeter = 10 millimeters, so 25 centimeters = 250 millimeters.

246. (C) You can find the answer by setting up a proportion: $\frac{1}{40} = 4.5/x$. Cross-multiplication leads to $x = 4.5(40)$, or $x = 180$ inches. Converting that to feet gets you an answer of $\frac{180}{12}$, or 15 feet.

247. (D) You should not need to compute if you estimate first. Your answer will be greater than 234 by around 23 + 2. The only possible answer is D.

248. (D) To divide fractions, invert the divisor and multiply. $\frac{7}{8} \div \frac{3}{8} = \frac{7}{8} \times \frac{8}{3}$. The answer is $\frac{7}{3}$, which simplified is $2\frac{1}{3}$.

249. (C) Take 2% of $1,050: 0.02 × $1,050 = $21. Now add that to $1,050: $1,050 + $21 = $1,071.

250. (120) If 60% showed improvement, 40% did not: 0.40 × 300 = 120.

251. (32) There are 16 cups in a gallon and 32 cups in 2 gallons.

252. (A) You know that Jake (J) is half as old as Tony (T), so T = 2J. You also know that Tony (2J) is 4 years younger than Q + J. You know that Q = 10, so you can now solve:

$$2J = 10 + J - 4$$

$$2J = 6 + J$$

$$J = 6$$

To check, plug in all the ages. Quinn is 10, Jake is 6, and Tony is 12.

253. (D) If she gets 2% quarterly, she gets 2% calculated four times a year. The first quarter, she ends up with $102. The second quarter, she makes 2% on $102, for a total of $104.04. The third quarter, she makes 2% on $104.04, for a total of $106.12. The fourth quarter, she makes 2% on $106.12, for a total of $108.24.

254. (11200) First find the number of calories daily: 2,000 − (0.2 × 2,000) = 1,600. Now multiply that by the number of days in a week: 1,600 × 7 = 11,200.

255. (A) There are 3 teaspoons in a tablespoon, so there are 9 teaspoons in 3 tablespoons.

256. (B) Estimating doesn't help much here, so just do the multiplication. 10.6 × 0.3 = 3.18. Alternatively, you can think:

$$0.3 × 10 = 3 \qquad\qquad 0.3 × 0.6 = 0.18$$

$$\downarrow \qquad\qquad\qquad\qquad \downarrow$$

$$3 \qquad\qquad\qquad + 0.18 = 3.18$$

257. (B) Divide 235 by 250 to find the percent Daniel got right. 235 ÷ 250 = 0.94, or 94%.

258. (A) Estimation should eliminate choices C and D, and looking at place value should show you that 43.210 − 1.234 will give you an answer whose last digit is 6, not 7. The correct answer is A.

259. (56) Solve this as you would any other problem of this sort. Think: $0.15x = 8.4$. $8.4 ÷ 0.15 = 56$. Check by thinking: Does it make sense that 15% of 56 would be around 8?

260. **(D)** Express the mixed number as an improper fraction: $^{17}/_3$. Then find the lowest common denominator and restate the two fractions: $^{119}/_{21} + {^{18}/_{21}}$. Solve, and express as a mixed number in lowest terms: $^{137}/_{21} = 6^{11}/_{21}$.

Chapter 5: Biology

261. **(B)** Enzymes in the saliva and duodenum break down carbohydrates into their basic units, monosaccharides, of which glucose is one.

262. **(A)** An autotroph can produce organic nutrients from inorganic substances such as carbon dioxide. Autotrophs use energy from light or inorganic chemical sources to convert simple substances into complex compounds. All green plants are autotrophs.

263. **(A)** The taxonomic categories in order from least to most specific are: kingdom, phylum, class, order, family, genus, species.

264. **(B)** Carbohydrates and lipids are made up of different combinations of carbon, hydrogen, and oxygen. Proteins are made up of amino acids, which center around carbon atoms and always contain hydrogen and oxygen plus nitrogen. Nucleic acids contain carbon, hydrogen, and oxygen in their simple sugars plus nitrogen and phosphates.

265. **(A)** Monerans are prokaryotic, and they do not have vacuoles, centrioles, mitochondria, lysosomes, endoplasmic reticula, nuclear membranes, or Golgi apparatuses.

266. **(D)** Transpiration is the process by which water is passively transported from into the roots of a plant and then moves through the xylem to the leaves, from which it evaporates.

267. **(C)** Of the animals listed, only birds reproduce through internal fertilization and have eggs that continue to develop outside the body.

268. **(A)** *Intrachromosomal* means "occurring within a chromosome." *Translocation* is a change in position of a chromosomal segment.

269. **(A)** Prokaryotes do have ribosomes (choice B), DNA (choice C), and cytoplasm (choice D). They lack membrane-bound organelles (choice A), which include mitochondria, chloroplasts, and vacuoles as well as nuclei.

270. **(B)** A parasitic relationship is one in which one organism benefits (in this case, the bacterium) to the detriment of another (in this case, the human).

271. **(D)** The Latin names by which we know certain animals are typically their genus and species names. In order, a housecat is from the kingdom Animalia, phylum Chordata, class Mammalia, order Carnivora, family Felidae, genus *Felis*, and species *catus*.

272. **(A)** Waxes, oils, and fats are lipids.

273. (C) The independent variable is the variable being manipulated by the students. In this case, it is the different media in which the fungi are being grown.

274. (D) Minerals are inorganic. Organic molecules are formed from carbon chains and include carbohydrates, proteins, lipids, and nucleic acids.

275. (B) The water concentration outside the cell will be greater than that within the cell, so osmosis will pull water from outside to inside the cell, eventually overfilling it to the point where it swells and bursts.

276. (C) Fermentation is an incomplete form of cellular respiration. When it occurs in yeast, pyruvic acid is converted into ethanol and carbon dioxide. When it occurs in muscle cells that are not receiving enough oxygen, pyruvic acid is converted into lactic acid.

277. (C) Telophase is the phase in which the spindle dissolves and new membranes and nucleoli form, leading to two new cells.

278. (B) In protein synthesis, coded information from DNA is translated into a finished protein. First, DNA unzips, and RNA nucleotides bond with bases on each unzipped segment, forming messenger RNA. Then messenger RNA leaves the nucleus and attaches to a ribosome in the cytoplasm. Transfer RNA moves into position along the messenger RNA, and the amino acids attached to the transfer RNA molecules bond, forming the protein.

279. (D) Flagella and cilia are hair-like appendages that project from a cell. Although they may be sensory, they are usually used in some kind of movement, from the gyrating motion of a bacterium to the sweeping motion in fallopian tubes that pushes the ovum toward the uterus.

280. (C) In order, dogs belong to the kingdom Animalia, the phylum Chordata, the class Mammalia, the order Carnivora, the family Canidae, the genus *Canis*, and the species *lupus*.

281. (A) In saturated fats, all carbons are attached to two hydrogen atoms.

282. (A) The centriole is involved in animal cell reproduction. Vacuoles (choice C) are found in plant cells but not in animal cells.

283. (C) A *reactant* is a substance that undergoes a change. In photosynthesis, the reactants are carbon dioxide and water.

284. (A) For structures to be homologous, they must not only be parallel in form and function but must also occur in animals with a common ancestor. Because sharks are fish and dolphins are mammals, their fins are not considered homologous (choice C). However, the similarities in form and function between the human arm and the whale flipper—both found in mammals—are enough to make scientists consider these structures homologous.

285. (B) ATP energizes glucose so that it can be broken down, and then the glucose molecules in the cytoplasm of the cell split in half, with each half of the six-carbon glucose becoming a three-carbon substance called pyruvic acid, releasing energy in the process in the form of ATP.

286. (D) Mitosis is cell division that produces new cells with the same number of chromosomes as the original cell. Meiosis (choice A) is the type of cell division that produces cells with half of the organism's normal chromosome number.

287. (A) RNA is ribonucleic acid; its sugar is ribose. DNA is deoxyribonucleic acid; its sugar is deoxyribose.

288. (C) Think about a coffee pot, or percolator. Percolation is a process of filtering water. In the water cycle, the water filters through soil into underground aquifers.

289. (C) Ecological succession refers to the changes in an ecosystem over time. In Canada, the result of succession, also known as the *climax community*, would most likely be dense forest and large, mature trees.

290. (D) The cytosol portion of the cytoplasm is formed from water, salts, and organic molecules. It makes up a large portion of the cell.

291. (B) To track "changing attitudes," researchers would need to talk to people.

292. (B) Gymnosperms include all of the conifers, which have needle-like leaves. Instead of being surrounded by a fruit, the seeds of such plants are naked, although they may be housed in cones.

293. (D) Pupfish are an example of the kind of mutations caused by geographic isolation that Darwin first noticed in Galapagos finches. Because the fish cannot move from pool to pool, they do not interbreed, and they develop differently over time.

294. (C) Cellular respiration breaks down glucose and oxygen into carbon dioxide and water, using ADP, which is composed of phosphates and adenosine.

295. (B) The measurement is reliable, because repeating it yields the same result. However, because it does not equal Patient A's true weight, it is not valid.

296. (C) The greatest energy content is at the base of the energy pyramid. A coyote, being a secondary consumer, is higher up the energy chain than any of the other choices.

297. (D) Unlike the other animals listed, the sponge lacks nervous, digestive, and circulatory systems. It is a very simple organism.

298. (D) The more measurements made, the more valid the data are likely to be. Using three sites rather than one allows the researcher to increase observations.

299. (C) This choice reduces the possibility that one brand might emit more radiation than another; it also allows for a before-and-after measurement that is parallel for each test.

300. (A) The greatest energy content is at the base of the food pyramid; therefore:

producers > primary consumers > secondary consumers > decomposers

An herbivore would be a primary consumer; carnivores and omnivores are more likely to be secondary consumers.

301. (C) The gene for the disease is recessive, so only homozygous recessive offspring *(aa)* manifest the disease. An offspring that carries the recessive gene along with the dominant *A* gene *(Aa)* will carry but not manifest the disease. In a Punnett square, this would mean two out of four offspring.

302. (C) While humans are born with lungs, frogs undergo a metamorphosis and change the way they exchange gases.

303. (A) Their hypothesis was that salt water would affect locomotion negatively (choice B), but the students failed to use anything to which to compare the effect of salt water. A more reasonable experiment might have used fresh water for one batch of hydra and salt water for another batch, or fresh water for one batch and different solutions of salt water for several other batches.

304. (A) Of the colors listed, the one best absorbed by chlorophyll is blue. Fluorescent grow lights produce a good deal of blue light.

305. (D) Most bacteria are spherical (choice D), rod-shaped (choice B), or spiral-shaped (choice C).

306. (A) In hydrolysis, any class of compound is broken down into subunits through the addition of water.

307. (C) Our chromosomes are usually the same in number (choice A), shape (choice B), and size (choice D). It is the sequence of certain nucleotides that determines our uniqueness.

308. (D) *Cohesion* is the attraction between like molecules. It enables water to move upward in a plant against the pull of gravity.

309. (D) Active transport usually involves molecules moving from lower concentration to higher concentration, or against the concentration gradient. This requires a form of energy, often from ATP.

310. (B) Enzymes are proteins that function as catalysts in chemical reactions.

311. (A) Gymnosperms do not produce flowers or encase their seeds in fruit. Evergreens and conifers are gymnosperms.

312. (C) This is the definition of commensalism. An example might be cattle egrets and cattle. The cattle stir up insects, and the egrets consume them.

313. (D) The sepal is the green part of a flower that surrounds the bud and later supports the flower.

314. (C) In the form of asexual reproduction known as *budding*, cell division at one point in the organism results in an outgrowth, or bud, that develops into a new organism. Sponges, hydra, flatworms, and coral use budding to create genetically identical offspring.

315. (B) Auxins get their name from a Greek word meaning "to grow." Auxins are involved in every aspect of plant growth, from embryo development to leaf formation. They are also involved in plant phototropism (choice A), creating elongated cells on the shaded side of a plant, which causes the plant to bend toward the sun.

316. (D) These beadlike organelles are located in the cytoplasm of nearly all cells, on the rough endoplasmic reticulum. They assemble the proteins that the cell uses to grow, repair itself, and control processes.

317. (C) The products of fermentation are ethanol and carbon dioxide. It is the latter that causes the dough to rise.

318. (B) Mitosis creates cells that are exact copies of each other, down to the number of chromosomes in the cell. Meiosis, which creates sex cells, forms cells with half the number of chromosomes in the original cell.

319. (D) You may be able to guess this one through the process of elimination. Angiosperms are flowering plants, and the gingko tree does not have flowers. Instead, although it does not resemble pines or firs, it is classified as a gymnosperm.

320. (D) The taiga is the snow forest of Canada, Alaska, Siberia, Scandinavia, northern Mongolia, northern Japan, and Iceland. It features coniferous forests of pines, spruces, and larches.

321. (C) The formula represents carbon dioxide pairing with water to form a simple sugar and oxygen. This is what happens in the process of photosynthesis.

322. (B) The students' measurements were precise, in that they corresponded closely with each other. However, since the true measurement differed from theirs by at least 0.13 g, the measurements were not terribly accurate.

323. (C) The greatest energy content is at the base of the energy pyramid, where the producers of energy congregate; therefore, producers > primary consumers > secondary consumers > decomposers.

324. (C) *Homo* is the human genus, which includes *Homo neanderthalensis*. *Homo sapiens* is the only living example of the genus.

325. (A) Phloem carries nutrients, especially sucrose. The nutrients are carried in a fluid called *sap* to the parts of the plant that need them.

Chapter 6: Chemistry

326. (D) Both acids contain hydrogen (choice C), as the prefix *hydro-* indicates. Because they have the prefix *hydro-* and the suffix *-ic*, they are binary acids (choice A), meaning that they are a combination of hydrogen with a second, nonmetallic element. It is those elements that differ from acid to acid.

327. (C) Process of elimination should help with this one. You should know that helium (He) is a gas, and silver (Ag) and zinc (Zn) are solids at room temperature. That leaves mercury (Hg), whose liquid properties make it useful for many purposes.

328. (A) Protons and neutrons have similar (though not identical) masses, and electrons are much smaller. An alpha particle (choice C) is made up of protons and neutrons. A beta particle (choice D) is a fast-moving electron.

329. (C) Isotopes are forms of the same element. They contain equal numbers of protons but different numbers of neutrons, making their masses different. The numerals 15 and 18 in O-15 and O-18 are mass numbers.

330. (B) When an electron absorbs additional energy from an outside source, it can move into an excited state, a higher energy level. To move back, it must release that energy.

331. (C) Aluminum as an atom has 13 electrons. For an aluminum ion to have a $+3$ charge indicates that the atom lost three electrons and now has ten.

332. (A) The pH scale has a range of 1 to 14 with the number 7 indicating a neutral solution. An acidic sample will have a lower pH value, whereas a basic solution will have a higher pH value. Blood with a pH of 1.3 would be considered strongly acidic.

333. (D) Forty years represent two half-lives. After one half-life, 3 grams will remain. After two, 1.5 grams will remain.

334. (C) Significant figures include all digits except leading zeroes or placeholder zeroes. Accuracy refers to the closeness of a measurement to its true value. In this case, the only significant figures are 3 and 1, and the measurement is accurate to 0.001 g.

335. (B) The rows in the table are periods. Elements in the same period have the same number of electron shells. Across a period from left to right, elements become less metallic.

336. (C) Calculate the number of neutrons by subtracting the atomic number from the mass number. The mass number of carbon-12 is 12, and the atomic number for carbon is 6, so $12 - 6 = 6$.

337. (C) The electron distribution of an atom is divided into shells, which in turn contain subshells composed of the orbitals in which the electrons reside. In electron configuration, the symbols 1s, 2s, 2p, and so on, are used to designate subshells, with superscripts indicating the number of electrons in each subshell. There is a maximum number of electrons per subshell. Magnesium has atomic number 12, meaning that it has 12 protons, and in its balanced state, 12 electrons. Looking at the superscripts alone should tell you that only the superscripts in choice C add up to 12.

338. (A) You need simply to divide the number of moles by the number of liters to determine the molarity: $^{0.45}/_4 = 0.1125$, which rounds to 0.11.

339. (C) Carbon's atomic mass is approximately 12.01 amu.

340. (A) A cation is an ion with fewer electrons than protons, making it positively charged.

341. (B) Helium has the lowest melting and boiling point. Carbon (choice A) has the highest melting point, and tungsten has the highest boiling point.

342. (B) Red litmus paper turns blue under alkaline (basic) conditions. Of the solutions given, only NaOH, sodium hydroxide, is alkaline. Choice A is table salt, which is essentially neutral. Choice C is nitric acid, and choice D is sulfuric acid.

343. (B) There are 58.5 grams in 1 mole of NaCl. Setting up to calculate the molarity of the solution, you divide 1.0 mole by 0.500 liters: 1.0 moles ÷ 0.500 liters = 2.0 M.

344. (D) Sodium nitrite is $NaNO_2$ (choice C). Sodium nitrate is $NaNO_3$. It is used in fertilizer and as a preservative.

345. (D) Ionization energy is the minimum energy required to remove one electron from each atom in a mole of atoms in a gaseous state. On the periodic table, ionization potential tends to increase across a period, because the greater number of protons (not neutrons) attract orbiting electrons more strongly, thus requiring more energy to remove those electrons from orbit.

346. (C) This combination of iron and sulfur forms iron (II) sulfide, and is a synthesis reaction.

347. (D) The ionization energy of an atom is the energy required to remove the outermost electron from the atom. This energy is needed to overcome the attraction between the positively charged protons and the negatively charged electrons.

348. (A) Molecular oxygen is O_2; ozone is O_3. It is thermodynamically unstable and highly reactive.

349. (B) The compound has four carbon atoms joined by single bonds, making it a molecule of butane.

350. (A) Hydrocarbons are formed of hydrogen and carbon. Complete combustion in oxygen forms CO_2 and H_2O.

351. (A) The zinc is balanced across the equation, but the chlorine and hydrogen are not. Choice A gives you two atoms of each on either side of the equation.

352. (C) On the periodic table, the atomic radii of atoms tend to decrease across a period from left to right and increase down a group, with the largest radii appearing in group I and at the bottoms of groups.

353. (D) Nearly all organic compounds contain a carbon-hydrogen bond. Of the compounds listed here, hydrochloric acid (choice A), ammonia (choice B), and carbon dioxide (choice C) are inorganic. Methane (choice D) is organic.

354. (D) Propane is a hydrocarbon, unlike the other choices on the list. Its formula is C_3H_8.

355. (C) Certain unstable atoms emit rays and thus change into atoms with a different chemical identity, a process known as radioactivity. Alpha rays consist of particles that carry a $+2$ charge.

356. (D) Chemical compounds are named in the order of the elements shown. Ag is silver, and NO3 is nitrate. Nitrates have three oxygen atoms; nitrites (choice C) have two.

357. (B) Oxidation numbers for atoms in a neutral molecule must add up to 0. Hydrogen has an oxidation number of $+1$ when combined with nonmetals and -1 when combined with metals. In this case, it is combined with a nonmetal, so to obtain a sum of 0, the chlorine atom must have an oxidation number of -1.

358. (D) This is an example of the double replacement reaction that occurs when aluminum nitrate and sulfuric acid react together.

359. (B) Metals make up about two-thirds of the periodic table and are mostly located on the left and center areas of the table. Nonmetals are located on the upper right side of the periodic table. Semimetals form a staircase that runs between metals and nonmetals on the periodic table.

360. (A) Set up a simple equation if it helps. Suppose that gas A has a molar mass of M1, and gas B has a molar mass four times that, M2. Now suppose that M1 = 1 and M2 = 4. The square root of $\frac{1}{4} = \frac{2}{1}$, so the rate of effusion for gas A is half that of gas B.

361. (A) Certain native metals are found in nature, either in alloy or pure forms. Gold (Au) is one such metal.

362. (D) A neutral sodium atom contains 11 protons and 11 electrons. Take one electron away, and you end up with a positively charged sodium ion (Na+) with a net charge of $+1$.

363. (D) Rusting is the oxidation of iron.

364. (C) A high melting point is typical of an element with very strong bonds. Of the metals listed, you can probably guess that iron is the strongest.

365. (A) The presence of covalent bonds in most organic molecules makes reaction time slower.

366. (B) Examination of the first substance shows that methane gas has one carbon atom. There is also one carbon atom on the right side of the equation, so there is no need to balance this. There are four hydrogen atoms on the left side. To balance this, change the coefficient on the right side so that there are four hydrogen atoms there as well:

$$\_CH_4 + \_O_2 \rightarrow \_CO_2 + 2H_2O$$

Now there are two atoms of oxygen on the left and four on the right (two from carbon dioxide and two from water). To balance, change the coefficient on the left to 2:

$$CH_4 + 2O_2 \rightarrow CO_2 + 2H_2O$$

367. (D) Reactivity is the tendency of an element to undergo chemical change, which in turn depends on its stability. Xenon, a noble gas, is extremely stable and thus nonreactive under normal conditions.

368. (D) Ionic compounds have high melting points, good conductivity, and a crystalline shape. An example is table salt, NaCl.

369. (D) The mass number is the sum of the protons and neutrons in the atom.

370. (A) Zn is zinc, and SO_4 is a sulfate. ZnS would be zinc sulfide (choice B). ZnO would be zinc oxide (choice D).

371. (A) With a few rare exceptions, oxygen has an oxidation number of -2 in a compound.

372. (B) Weak intermolecular forces have a low boiling point. Strong intermolecular forces have a high boiling point.

London dispersion < dipole–dipole < H-bonding < ion-ion

London dispersion is the weakest force of those shown. (A Keesom interaction is one form of dipole–dipole interaction.)

373. (D) At room temperature, fluorine and chlorine are toxic gases. Iodine is a solid. Bromine is a liquid.

374. (D) Heating affects solubility of most solvents. Solubility increases with heat for most substances, but may decrease for gases. Pressure (choice C) affects only the solubility of gases. Stirring (choice B) may affect the speed of solubility of some substances (for example, sugar in tea). Of the choices, only heating has an effect in every instance.

375. (C) Most metals conduct electricity well, because they contain a number of free electrons that move around easily and can therefore easily carry electric current.

376. (C) Water freezes at 0°C. Water with salt in it freezes at a slightly lower temperature. Therefore, putting salt onto melting ice will keep that melting ice from refreezing. As more salt is added, the freezing point of the water is further reduced.

377. (B) Metals typically have excess electrons, whereas nonmetals have a few fewer electrons than are needed for stability. When they combine, the metals lose electrons, forming cations (positive ions). The nonmetals gain electrons, forming anions (negative ions). The cations and anions then merge, and the compound is named with the cation first and the anion with an *–ide* suffix second. Examples include sodium chloride or zinc oxide.

378. (D) If the elements in a covalent bond have different electronegativity values, the unequal sharing of electrons causes the bond to be polar. H_2O is the only choice with a polar covalent bond.

379. (B) This type of equation represents decomposition, the breaking down of a compound into its component parts.

380. (C) Sulfur is located on the upper right side of the periodic table. It is soft, lacks luster, and does not conduct heat or electricity well, making it a nonmetal.

Chapter 7: Anatomy and Physiology

381. (D) Although an ectopic pregnancy may occur anywhere outside the uterus, it is most likely to involve implantation in one of the tubes that carries eggs from the ovaries to the uterus. In such a case, it may be referred to as a tubal pregnancy, although it is not viable and cannot proceed.

382. (D) Thyroxine (T4) aids in the regulation of metabolism.

383. (D) Because of the hyperflexion and hyperextension caused by such a collision, it is not uncommon to find tears or stretching of the ligaments of the spine. The injury is front-to-back, making choice B unlikely, and a herniated disc (choice C) is more of a compression injury.

384. (C) Defecation (choice A) is the elimination of waste. Osmosis (choice B) is the movement of molecules across a membrane. Circulation (choice D) is the movement of blood through the body. Peristalsis (choice C) is the involuntary, wavelike movement of muscles in the intestine and elsewhere that pushes food along.

385. (A) Some nutrients supply energy, and others support metabolism. Nutrients in the first set include carbohydrates, proteins, and fats. Those in the second set include vitamins, minerals, and water.

386. (A) The exchange of oxygen and carbon dioxide takes place between the alveoli and the capillaries of the circulatory system. The alveoli are tiny air sacs that form the terminus of the bronchioles.

387. (B) FSH (choice A) and LH (choice C) regulate reproduction. ADH (choice D) promotes water retention. TRH (choice B) is produced in the hypothalamus and releases thyroid-stimulating hormone.

388. (C) The ribs are in front of the lungs in the human body, making them closer to the front of the body, or anterior.

389. (B) The range is about 7.35 to 7.45, making blood fairly neutral. Excess carbon dioxide can lead to acidosis, a pH below 7.35.

390. (C) The cerebellum lies below the cerebrum and is responsible for various aspects of motor control.

391. (D) Lactase breaks down lactose into simpler sugars.

392. (B) The hypothalamus regulates the body's internal balance, or homeostasis. It also controls the pituitary gland and links the endocrine system to the nervous system.

393. (A) Fluid balance is connected to electrolyte balance. The key electrolytes in the human body include sodium, potassium, calcium, chloride, and bicarbonate.

394. (A) The pineal gland, located in the brain, produces melatonin, which controls sleep patterns and circadian rhythm. The pituitary gland stimulates growth (choice B), the mammary gland produces milk (choice C), and the adrenal glands produce corticosteroids, which may reduce inflammation (choice D).

395. (D) The disease known as rickets is a product of vitamin D deficiency and results in the softening and bending of bones.

396. (B) One of the jobs of the lymphatic system is to prevent excess fluid from accumulating in tissues by collecting it and moving it into the circulatory system via the brachiocephalic veins.

397. (D) The parathyroid hormone regulates calcium in the body through several means, one of which is increasing the production of activated vitamin D.

398. (B) An electrolyte is a substance that dissociates into ions in a solution, thus becoming conductive and enabling the flow of water molecules across cell membranes. Potassium (choice A), sodium (choice C), calcium (choice D), phosphate, chloride, magnesium, bicarbonate, and sulfate are the major electrolytes used by the body.

399. (C) The hair follicles are housed deeper, in the dermis.

400. (D) The axial skeletal system is the system of bones in the head and torso, encompassing the skull, spinal column, sternum, and ribs. The radius (choice D) is a bone in the arm.

401. (C) The gall bladder stores the fat-digesting bile produced by the liver.

402. (D) In nonspecific immunity, the response is immediate and antigen-independent, meaning that the invading organism need not be identified by the body. In specific immunity, the response takes some time and is antigen-dependent, as the production of specific antibodies would be.

403. (D) Although iron is vital for red blood formation, copper is important for proper iron metabolism. A copper deficiency can quickly lead to anemia.

404. (C) The dorsal body cavity contains the spinal column, making it posterior, or toward the back of the body, compared to the ventral body cavity, which contains the structures of the chest and abdomen.

405. (B) The integumentary system (the skin and its appendages) waterproofs the body from outside and guards against excess fluid loss from inside.

406. (A) The clavicle, or collarbone, juts horizontally between the sternum and scapula (shoulder blade). It connects the arms to the body.

407. (C) Both rods and cones are photoreceptors, but rods are more sensitive to low light and are thus critical to night vision.

408. (B) When air builds up in the cavity that holds the lungs, due to a chest injury or other cause, it can put pressure on the lungs and interfere with breathing.

409. (C) Damage to a disc in the lower back will most likely cause pain radiating downward along the sciatic nerve.

410. (B) The ulna (choice A), radius (choice C), and humerus (choice D) are arm bones.

411. (D) The ovaries are the egg-producing reproductive organs.

412. (D) The zygomatic bone is a rhombus-shaped bone that forms the base of the eye orbit and the bulge of the cheek.

413. (B) Urea is a crystalline compound that results from protein metabolism in humans and other mammals. It is excreted in the urine.

414. (D) Any ring of muscle that serves to close and open a tubal structure may be called a *sphincter*. The talus is the anklebone, not a tubal structure.

415. (B) The microscopic study of tissues is histology. The other responses refer to hematology (choice A), cardiology (choice C), and symptomatology (choice D).

416. (A) The corpus callosum is a broad band of nerve fibers that joins the two hemispheres of the brain.

417. (C) The integumentary system includes the skin, hair, nails, and assorted glands. Receptors embedded in the skin receive information regarding heat, pain, air flow, and so on, which transports through the nervous system to the brain.

418. (C) The two valves connect the heart to the pulmonary artery and the aorta, which carry blood from the heart to the rest of the body.

419. (A) The bicep both flexes and supinates (turns) the forearm.

420. (D) Chyle is formed by the small intestine as fatty food is digested. The fat globules in the lymph travel via the lymphatic system to the bloodstream by way of an opening in the thoracic duct.

421. (D) The duodenum is the initial section of the small intestine; the pancreatic and bile ducts empty into it.

422. (C) Tears (choice A), urine (choice B), and mucus (choice D) are all primary lines of defense, because they work to prevent infection. Inflammation (choice C) is an example of a secondary line of defense, because it kicks in once the body has been infected.

423. (A) Bone tissue stores a variety of minerals, from calcium to phosphorus, releasing them into the bloodstream as needed.

424. (A) Deoxygenated blood first enters the heart via the right atrium.

425. (A) The synapse is the junction between the terminal of one neuron and the next (or between a neuron and a muscle or gland cell).

426. (C) The primary genitalia are those that are external and visible. In a female human, that would include the clitoris, labia, and vulva.

427. (D) Epinephrine is also known as adrenaline. It is typically released in times of stress.

428. (D) The calcaneus, or heel bone, is not directly analogous to anything in the hand. The phalanges (choice A), or toe bones, are analogous to the phalanges, or finger bones, and the metatarsal and tarsal in the foot (choices B and C) are analogous to the metacarpal and carpal in the hand.

429. (B) The limbic system of structures in the brain controls a variety of functions, including emotions, behavior, long-term memory, and the sense of smell. The medulla oblongata is the lower part of the brain stem and controls several involuntary functions, including breathing and heart rate.

430. (A) A sagittal section occurs along a longitudinal plane, dividing the body into right and left regions.

431. (A) Something that is anterior is toward the front of the body. The nose is the most anterior feature on the list of choices.

432. (A) The diaphragm is a sheet of muscle that divides the thoracic cavity (containing the heart, esophagus, and lungs) from the abdominal cavity (containing the stomach, spleen, and kidneys).

433. (A) A goiter may put pressure on the trachea and esophagus, causing difficulty in breathing or swallowing.

434. (C) The stirrup is the final bone in the middle ear. Sound waves compress it, and it in turn compresses the waves so that they may be moved to the inner ear.

435. (D) Hemoglobin is a red protein that transports oxygen. Oxygen is not very soluble in water, which is the main component of blood, so the body uses the four iron ions in molecules of hemoglobin to bind to four O_2 molecules. This iron gives hemoglobin and thus red blood cells their color.

436. (B) T4, or thyroxine, is the main hormone manufactured by the thyroid. It is named T4 because it contains four iodine ions per molecule.

437. (C) Smooth muscle is involuntary muscle. It is found in blood vessels; lymphatic vessels; the reproductive, respiratory, and gastrointestinal tracts; and the iris of the eye, among other locations.

438. (D) The main function of the valves is to prevent blood from flowing backward.

439. (B) The average person in good health has a pulse of about 72 beats per minute and a blood pressure of 120 over 80 mm Hg.

440. (A) The nares are the nostrils.

441. (A) Pepsin aids chemical digestion in the stomach by breaking down proteins.

442. (C) All of the bones listed are part of the skull, but the cranium and mandible form the two main parts. The cranium encloses the brain, and the mandible is the jaw bone.

443. (B) Of the choices given, fasciae (choice A) connect muscles to muscles, ligaments (choice C) connect bone to bone, and cartilage (choice D) may connect the surfaces of a joint.

444. (A) Collagen is the protein that forms the structure of most connective tissue in the body. It may be found in skin, tendons, ligaments, cartilage, bones, blood vessels, and the dentin in teeth.

445. (B) A certain amount of insulin is always being secreted, but as glucose rises, the level of insulin rises, and as glucose falls, the level of insulin falls. In response to the insulin, cells in the body absorb glucose from the blood.

Chapter 8: Physics

446. (A) Although the force will vary depending on the mass and velocity of the ball, the forces will be equal and opposite, per Newton's Third Law.

447. (B) A photon is a discrete bundle, or quantum, of electromagnetic energy.

448. (A) In free fall, the force acting on the object is gravity, and the acceleration of any object of any mass is constant at 9.8 m/s^2 (on Earth). The velocity of the object increases at a constant rate.

449. (C) When force and displacement work in the same direction, we call that "positive work." The other responses are examples of "negative work."

450. (D) Your radio plucks the frequency it wants out of thousands of frequencies in the air because its inductor and capacitor form a resonant circuit. They set a particular rate for current to flow into the system. They absorb the other frequencies and let the desired frequency affect the oscillator.

451. (C) Using this formula, energy is often measured in kilowatt-hours. For example, if you use a 100-watt light bulb 12 hours a day for 30 days, you will have used 100 × 360 watt-hours, or 36 kilowatt-hours.

452. (B) Force equals the extension of the spring times a constant ($F = dk$). If a force of 12 kg stretches this particular spring 3 cm, the constant is 4. Apply that same constant to the increased force: 30 = d × 4. The distance of the extension must be 30 ÷ 4, or 7.5 cm.

453. (C) Acceleration equals the speed squared divided by the radius: $a = v^2/R$. In this case, a = 4 m/s^2, and v = 10 m/s, so the radius must be 100 ÷ 4, or 25 m. The mass of the car is irrelevant to the problem.

454. (B) Charging with friction results in two objects with opposite charges. If the cup is positive, the cotton must now be negative—it has gained electrons and has a negative charge.

455. (A) Increasing distance by a factor of 2 decreases the force by a factor of 2^2, or 4. The new force of attraction is the original force divided by 4, or 3 units.

456. (D) The switch interrupts the electrical circuit or allows the current to flow from one conductor to another.

457. (C) Gay-Lussac's Law states that temperature and pressure are directly proportional. Heat from friction caused as tires rub on the road increases the temperature of the air in the tire, causing an increase in pressure. This is why you are advised to measure the pressure in your tires when they are cold—before starting a trip.

458. (C) The coulomb is the equivalent of one ampere-second. It is the base unit of electrical charge.

459. (A) The period is the time it takes for an event to repeat itself, measured in seconds. If the wings beat at 25 beats per second, the period of each wing beat is ½₅ of a second, or 0.04 s.

460. (C) Kinetic energy can be found using this formula: $KE = \frac{1}{2} m(v^2)$, where m = mass and v = speed. In this problem, that would be $\frac{1}{2}$ (500 × 100), or 2.5×10^4 Joules.

461. (B) Because the specific heat capacity of iron is close to twice that of tin, iron would require about twice as much heat to increase 1°C in temperature.

462. (B) Mass does not change from place to place. The astronaut's weight on Jupiter, on the other hand, would be over 215 kg (choice D).

463. (B) Friction is directly proportional to force on an object, and force is greater when weight is greater.

464. (C) The velocity of the car is equal to the time multiplied by the acceleration.

465. (D) An impulse is a change in momentum. The 10-kg object had a change in its velocity of 10 m/s. Using the equation "change in momentum equals mass times change in velocity," or $\Delta p = m\Delta v$, you can see that the answer is 100 kg·m/s.

466. (C) Increasing the temperature of a substance increases its volume and decreases its density. Such changes are far more evident in gases than in liquids or solids.

467. (B) A lot happens as a bat hits a ball in terms of momentum, direction, and velocity. In the case of acceleration, the force accelerates both objects, but the ball experiences a greater acceleration due to its smaller mass.

468. (D) Generally, you may think of light vibrating in multiple directions. Polarization filters, reflects, refracts, or scatters light so that the vibrations occur in a single plane.

469. (D) Doubling speed, or velocity, doubles momentum (choice D) and quadruples kinetic energy (choice B). The equation for this is $mv^2/2 = KE$.

470. (B) Water is close to perfectly transparent to visible light, but it scatters and reflects a good deal of ultraviolet light.

471. (B) Jacques Charles determined in 1787 that $V_1/T_1 = V_2/T_2$: for an ideal gas at constant pressure, volume is directly proportional to absolute temperature.

472. (C) The vibrations in longitudinal waves move parallel to the wave.

473. (A) Only choice A has both direction and magnitude, making it a vector.

474. (D) Fresh water has a density of around 1,000 kg/m^3, whereas that of salt water is around 1,030 kg/m^3. The difference in density of the fluids makes objects in salt water more buoyant than those in fresh water.

475. (C) A lightning rod is a pointed metal rod attached to a building or other structure. It provides a low-resistance path to ground that keeps lightning from damaging the structure.

The rod is usually connected to a wire that leads below ground to a ground rod or grid that allows the energy of a lightning strike to dissipate harmlessly.

476. (A) The spring's force is equivalent on both blocks, but the blocks' mass affects the speed of their movement. Think: 4 kg(3 m/s) = 6 kg(2 m/s).

477. (C) When light moves from a less dense to a denser substance, it refracts, or bends, because it changes speed as it hits the denser substance.

478. (D) The formula is simple: $S = D/T$.

479. (C) A kelvin is the same size as a degree Celsius, but in kelvins, 0° represents absolute zero. The boiling point of water is around 373 K, and the freezing point is 100 degrees below that, or around 273 K.

480. (B) In art class, you may learn the primary colors as blue, yellow, and red, but in physics, the primary colors are red, green, and blue, and the secondary colors are yellow, cyan, and magenta. Adding red, green, and blue light in equal intensities produces white light.

481. (B) Cork has holes throughout that reduce the volume of matter present (the cork is replaced by air), making it less dense than many other materials.

482. (D) Marilyn made a round trip of 8 miles to return to her starting point. Then she drove 1 mile plus 5 miles for a total of 6 miles to the wedding. Her displacement is 6 miles—the distance from her home to the wedding—but she drove a total distance of 14 miles.

483. (C) As long as the mass of the object remains the same, the relationship between force and acceleration is direct. Doubling the force will double the acceleration.

484. (B) Archimedes determined that the ratio of the output force to the input force (also known as the mechanical advantage) of a lever was equivalent to the distance from the fulcrum to the output force divided by the distance from the fulcrum to the input force, in this case 20/10, or 2.

485. (B) An object that is accelerating is changing either the magnitude or direction of its velocity vector. In the case of a rotating object, it is the direction that changes. Since time is part of the acceleration formula ($a = \Delta v/t$), it may help to think about the time in which each spec rotates, given the constant rate. The travel time for a rotation of each speck is the distance traveled divided by the speed. The speck on the edge travels further, so its time is greater. Since Δv is the same for both specks, the speck closer to the spindle has the greater acceleration.

486. (B) The speed of light varies slightly depending on the medium in which it travels. In a dense medium, it travels more slowly. Of the media given, glass is densest.

487. (D) A transformer consists of a primary and a secondary coil, with the primary coil attached to a source of AC voltage. The change in the magnetic field created by the primary coil induces voltage in the secondary coil. When the primary coil has more turns than the secondary coil, the combination reduces voltage and is called a "step-down" transformer. When the primary coil has fewer turns than the secondary coil, the combination increases voltage and is called a "step-up" transformer. As the voltage decreases, the current increases, and vice versa.

488. (D) With a plane mirror, the distance from an object to the mirror is identical to the distance from the mirror to the image.

489. (B) The period is 5 seconds. From that you can determine the frequency; it is the reciprocal of the period, or $\frac{1}{5}$. The wavelength is 9 meters. Knowing that and the frequency, you can determine the speed using the equation $v = f\lambda$: $\frac{1}{5}(9) = \frac{9}{5}$, or 1.8 m/s.

490. (C) Multiply velocity by mass to find momentum. 4.5 m/s $\times$ 5.5 kg = 24.75 kg·m/s.

491. (C) In a uniform magnetic field, the force is always at right angles to the motion of an electron, resulting in the electron's circular path.

492. (C) Heat may travel by convection through liquids or gases, but it travels only by conduction through solids.

493. (A) Determine the acceleration by dividing the speed squared by the radius of the track: $a = v^2/R$. In this case, $a = \frac{100}{50}$, or 2 m/s^2.

494. (A) According to Ohm's Law, current (I) equals voltage (ΔV) divided by resistance (R), or $I = \Delta V/R$. In this case, you know voltage and resistance, so $I = \frac{3}{60}$, or 0.05 amp.

495. (B) Use Coulomb's Law to find the force. The equation to use is this:

$$F_{elect} = \frac{k \times Q_1 \times Q_2}{d^2}$$

Remember that 1 coulomb = 10^6 microcoulombs. Both balloons in this problem have the same charge, so Q_1 and Q_2 in this case equal 5×10^{-6} C, and d, distance, = 25 cm, or 0.25 m. Now, you must recall Coulomb's constant, $k = (9.0 \times 10^9$ N·m^2/C^2). From this point, it's all about computation:

$$F_{elect} = \frac{9.0 \times 10^9 \text{ N·m}^2/\cancel{C}^2 \times (5 \times 10^{-6}\cancel{C}) \times (5 \times 10^{-6}\cancel{C})}{(0.25 \text{ m})^2} = \frac{225 \times 10^{-3}}{0.0125} = 1.8 \text{ N}$$

496. (D) A substance's half-life is the time it takes for the substance to decay to half its value. If the substance decays by half in 10 years, it will be half of one-half ($\frac{1}{4}$) in 20 years and half of that ($\frac{1}{8}$) in 30 years.

497. (C) Applying Newton's Second Law, $F = ma$, a 1.0-kg block accelerated at 6 m/s^2 requires a 6-N force to move it.

498. (A) The equation $P = IV$, power equals current times voltage, is the one to use. Dividing the power by the voltage gives you $I = P/V$, and 60 watts/110 volts equals approximately 0.55 amperes.

499. (A) According to the equation $v = f\lambda$, frequency is equal to the velocity of the wave divided by the wavelength. Dividing 20 m/s by 4 m gives you 5 s^{-1}.

500. (D) Plane mirrors have a magnification equal to 1; the dimensions of the image are equal to the dimensions of the object. The image has left-right reversal but is not inverted top to bottom.

NOTES